A CAR DEALER'S GUIDE TO GOOGLE ANALYTICS 4

Second Edition

A CAR DEALER'S GUIDE TO GOOGLE ANALYTICS 4

Second Edition

GEORGE NENNI

My sincere thanks to everyone who helped to make this book a success, especially the following:

Stephanie Nenni, my wife, for her support and patience over the many hours I spent putting this book together.

Suzanne Nenni Hull, my sister, who was a tremendous help in collecting Google Analytics 4 research and best practices.

My parents, Rudy and JoAnne Nenni, who taught me to work hard, play hard, and love hard.

TABLE OF CONTENTS

INTRODUCTION

Google Analytics 4 is the Future

Google Analytics is a website tracking and reporting service offered by Google. It was launched in November 2005 after Google acquired Urchin. The current Google Analytics Universal (or just Universal) has been around since October 2012, and the newest Google Analytics 4 (GA4) has been available since July 2019 (formerly known as "App + Web"). Both versions have run in parallel since late 2019.

Some version of Google Analytics is installed onto nearly every automotive dealership website across the world. Many dealers rely on the monthly reporting that comes directly or indirectly from Google Analytics. The tools allow dealers to track their website traffic, their paid campaigns, shopping behavior and true conversions such as lead forms, chat messages, phone calls, and digital retailing leads.

Google announced on March 16, 2022 that Analytics Universal will stop recording new data after July 1, 2023. That date came and went but, for most car dealers, their GA Universal data continued to flow until mid to late August 2023. Nevertheless, once Google stops collecting new data in Universal, they've announced they will still allow the collected data to be viewed until at least July 1, 2024. Currently, any remaining Google Analtyics Universal users must switch over to Google Analytics 4. The required rapid switchover has lit a fire under nearly every automotive digital marketing agency as well as website and tool providers. The good news is that the new Google Analytics 4 (GA4) is more powerful and easier to use.

Google Analytics 4 takes a fresh look at analytics and moves away from page-based measurement. Instead, it is centered around event-based measurement. GA4 is 100 percent event based, and it has a fundamental theory that any website or app interaction can be captured as an event. There are also a number of default events that are built into the reporting in order to have deeper insight into shopping behavior. GA4 will also experience fewer issues of spikes in spammy traffic because the new data stream approach only allows permissible and actual website data. The reporting built into GA4 is also much more intuitive and flexible, allowing a more visual approach to report building. Finally, GA4 promises to offer more insight into a car shopper's buying journey by showing the high-funnel, mid-funnel, and lower-funnel traffic sources and touch points that lead to conversions.

This book will guide the current or new Google Analytics user through the process of setting up Google Analtyics 4 (GA4), installing the code onto a dealership website, setting up the proper tracking, and generating actionable reporting.

GETTING STARTED

Google Analytics 4 versus Universal Analytics

As mentioned in the Introduction, Google Analytics 4 (GA4) takes a fresh approach to website and app analytics, and it moves to a 100 percent event-based platform. Google also includes a number of default events that measure traffic engagement and quality while doing away with metrics such as bounce rate, pages per session, and average session duration. This allows for more accurate and simplified reporting. Google recently added back a revised bounce rate to GA4, which is now simply the inverse of engagement rate.

GA4 also changes the approach to measuring users and sessions. The system tracks the source by which the user first arrived at the website, and it tracks the number of active users. GA4 also tracks all subsequent sessions, engaged sessions, and potential conversions for those users. This new dynamic means the GA4 user must be careful to choose the right dimensions and metrics, depending on whether they want to measure users or overall session volume. For instance, it will be helpful for dealers to understand the traffic sources or campaigns that are first delivering a user to their page. Dealers need to look at the influences along the shopping journey that end in a conversion. It will also be helpful for dealers to inspect which traffic sources are driving the most sessions and conversions without regard to first visits.

Building goals has also gotten much easier. They are now called conversions, and they are also 100 percent event based. Google has also increased the number of goals/conversions from the current twenty in Universal to thirty in GA4. As mentioned above, as GA4 breaks out users versus sessions more intentionally, GA4 users can be reported on for either session conversion rate or user conversion rate.

One significant challenge presented with GA4 is data thresholding where Google actually filters out traffic and events based on very low volume. If users find that some events or traffic is missing from their GA4 reports, that could be due to Google Analytics applying a data threshold. These thresholds are used to protect the privacy of individual users by preventing the assumption of their identities from demographics, interests, or other signals in the data. We'll discuss GA4 data thresholding later, and we'll show users how they can work around this.

In addition, there are also a number of metrics, default channel groupings, and other changes made in GA4.

Here is a rundown of some of the biggest changes in metrics:

Metric	Google Analytics Universal	Google Analytics 4
Active Users	N/A. GA Universal only had Users, which will be higher than Active Users.	Website shoppers that have been active within the last twenty-eight days. Will be lower than past User counts in Universal.
Average Session Duration	Average length of a session, from when a visitor lands on the first page of a dealer website to when they leave.	Replaced with Average Engagement Time per Session which promises to offer a more accurate measurement
Bounce Rate	The percentage of single-page sessions in which there was no interaction with the page.	A simple inverse of the Engagement Rate. For example, if engagement rate is 42%, bounce rate will be 58%.
Conversions/Goals	Called Goals in Universal. Tracked based on page views or events. One weakness of Universal has always been that it counts only one conversion per session for each goal. For example, vehicle detail page (VDP) goals would only count one VDP per session, even if the user viewed 5 VDPs.	Called Conversions in GA4, and 100 percent based on events. GA4 counts each and every conversion event, even if the same session triggers the same repeated conversion event. GA4 offers both user conversion rates and session conversion rates.
Engagement Rate	N/A. Instead, GA Universal used bounce rate, pages per session, session duration.	Percentage of sessions that lasted longer than ten seconds, had any conversion event, or had at least two page views. The ten second default can be changed in the Stream setup. Bounce rate is now the opposite of engagement rate.
Session	If User is on website when midnight arrives, a new session will be counted. If a User session connects with new source/medium/campaign parameters while on dealer website, a new session is started.	Sessions not restarted at midnight or when new source/medium/campaign parameters are connected.

Create Tracking Code for GA4

In order to begin using Google Analytics 4, a tracking code needs to be created and sent to the dealership's website provider. In order to do that, a Google Analytics account must first be active.

The goal for a dealership is to get GA4 tracking code installed on their website so that it will run in parallel to the existing GA Universal tracking code. When the current GA Universal stops collecting data on July 1, 2023, the dealership will simply switch over to the GA4 analytics system. The earlier a dealer starts this process, the more historical data they will have collected.

If there is no existing Google Analytics Universal system installed on a dealer website, which would be rare, or if the dealership doesn't own their Google Analytics (GA) and wishes to create a brand-new install, then a new Google Analytics property must first be created.

For a New Google Analytics System

When there is no existing Google Analytics system at a dealership and they want to install GA4, they may not know if they have an existing Google Account for the creation of GA4. Such a Google account could be any Gmail, Google Drive, or Google Photos account the dealer uses.

Our best practice advice is for a dealership to create a generic Gmail/Google account that will have admin rights to their Google Analytics. The account would not be tied to an individual. It would be a generic account such as NenniChevroletAnalytics@gmail.com. By creating a generic email account, a dealership can easily recover their Google Analytics access if a key employee with GA4 access leaves their job. Here is an example of creating a generic Google account for a dealership:

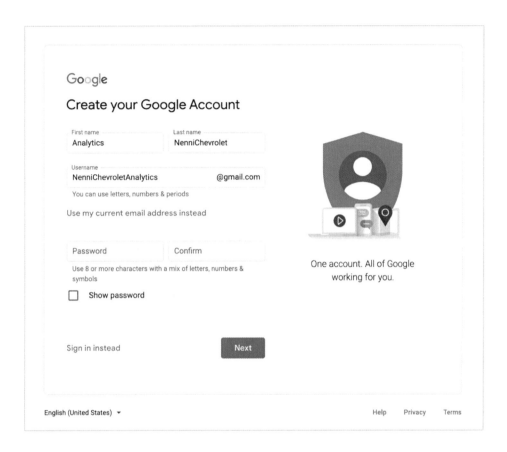

Once a new Google account is created, a user should go to https://analytics.google.com and they will be taken to the following screen:

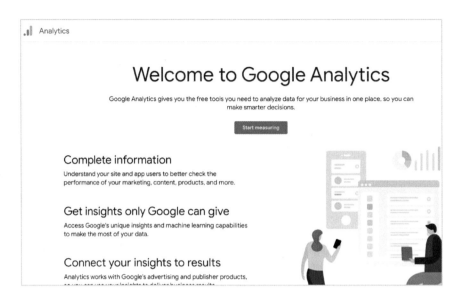

The user should click on Start measuring in the blue box. The system will then prompt the user to enter an account name. The dealer should be thoughtful about their approach to account naming and keep in mind that the account name is not the website property name. It is the owner account. If the Nenni family owns a Chevrolet, Ford, and CDJR dealership, the account name might be Nenni Auto Group, and then each property would be Nenni Chevrolet, Nenni Ford, and Nenni CDJR.

In addition, a dealer should make sure to check the box for Google Products and Services.

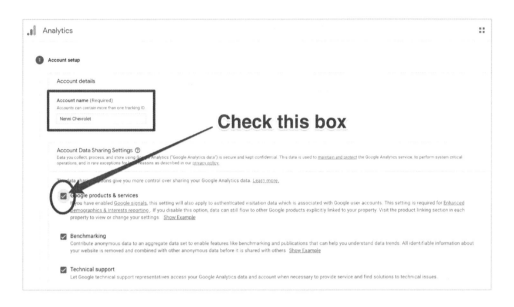

After clicking the Next button at the bottom of the screen, the user will be taken to the following screen:

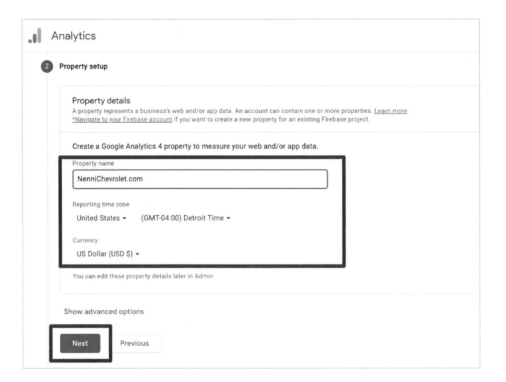

The dealer should enter the appropriate website property name, as well as choosing the right time zone and currency. Once the correct data is entered, the user should select the Next button.

On the next screen, the system will request the business size as well as the intended usage of Google Analytics, helping Google to tailor the experience. After entering that information, the user should click the Create button.

After agreeing to the terms of service in the following screen, the system will then open the new GA4 account.

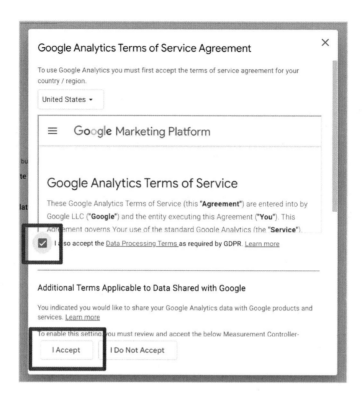

When the new GA4 account is created, the following screen will appear:

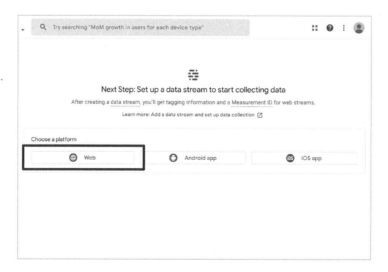

The proper selection for tracking dealer websites in GA4 would be the Web choice as shown above. Once Web is selected, the user is taken to the next screen:

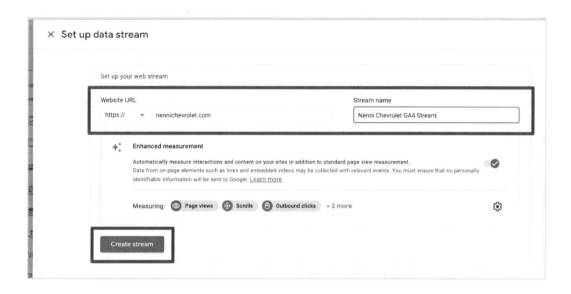

The dealer should enter their website URL and the GA4 stream name. We recommend including GA4 in the stream name to make it easy to find for future applications. Once the appropriate information is entered, the user should click on the Create stream button. The GA4 stream will then be created, and the user will be taken to the following screen:

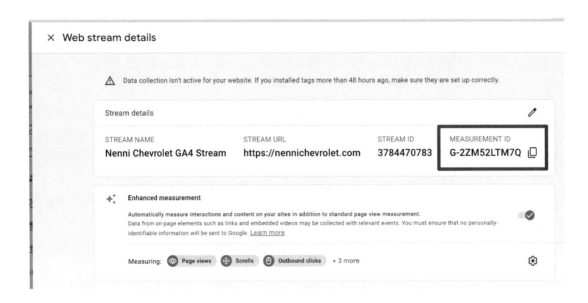

The most important element on this screen is the Measurement ID which starts with G and is followed by an alpha numeric combination. This is the ID the dealership should send to their website provider in order to get GA4 properly installed. It is the new GA4 tracking code that was created.

Converting Google Analytics Universal to Google Analytics 4

If a dealership already has a Google Analytics Universal account, and they wish to create a GA4 tracking code, there is an automatic GA4 Setup Assistant that will help. For that, a user should go to https://analytics.google.com.

To begin converting from Google Analytics Universal to Google Analytics 4, log in to Google Analytics Universal and go to the admin menu. You need to make sure your permission level is high enough because you will need account level access with the editor permission level.

After logging into a Google account, the user is taken to the following screen:

Once logged into Google Analytics Universal, the user should select the admin menu by clicking in the lower left-hand corner of the screen. After selecting the admin menu, the user is taken to the following screen, and they should choose GA4 Setup Assistant in the middle column.

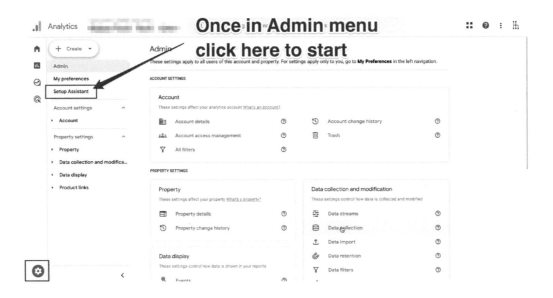

Once the user selects GA4 Setup Assistant, they are taken to the next screen. If the GA4 tracking code setup has not yet occurred, the screen should indicate Not Connected as shown in the screenshot.

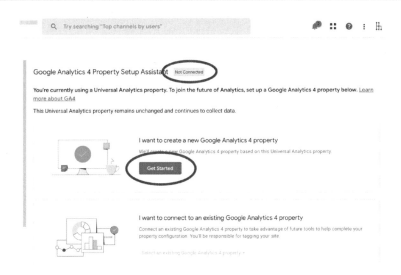

If a new GA4 tracking code is displaying as being connected, the GA4 tracking code was already created. Keep in mind, it does not mean that the new GA4 tracking code is live on the dealership website and that the data stream is flowing. It only means that the GA4 tracking has been created, and it needs to be sent to the dealer's website provider.

If the screen shows Not Connected, the user should click on the Get Started button. Once that button is clicked, the following screen appears. There will be a selection box where Google Analytics 4 can migrate the existing event tags from Google Analytics Universal. For nearly every automotive website provider, that box will be grayed out since those website providers use their own JavaScript libraries that won't automatically convert to GA4 format. This discussion does not need to get too technical because eventually all of the website and third-party website tool providers will offer GA4-compatible events. The bottom line is that a dealership should not click the box. They should leave it empty. The next step is to click the Create Property button.

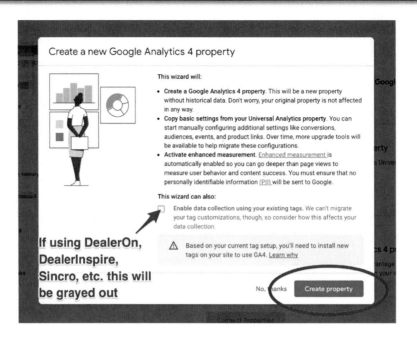

After selecting the Create Property button, the user should see the following confirmation screen showing that the GA4 tracking code has been successfully created. Clicking the button for See your GA4 property, will open a new browser window for the new GA4 property.

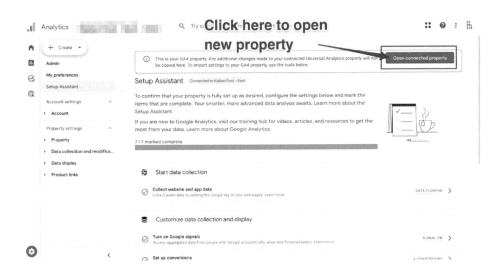

Whether the user created a brand-new GA4 account, or whether they used the GA4 Setup Assistant, the next step is to first change some default settings and then send the tracking code to the automotive website provider.

Changing GA4 Default Settings

Creating a new GA4 property is the first step in migrating from Universal analytics. In addition, we recommend changing a few default settings in order to optimize reporting.

Google Signals:

Google signals is website traffic that Google links to users who are signed in to their Google accounts and have Ads Personalization activated. This connected data with these logged-in users allows cross-device reporting, cross-device retargeting, and the export of cross-device conversions for paid search integration in Google Ads.

Note: Turning on Google Signals will make the Google Analytics 4 property subject to data thresholding. Data thresholding in GA4 is a privacy protection feature. It hides some data in reports in order to keep the identities of users private, especially when there aren't many users in a report. Data thresholding is covered later in this book in more depth. Ultimately, the benefits of Google Signals outweigh the data thresholding downsides. More sophisticated dealers and groups can work around data thresholding by utilizing Big Query although programming expertise is required.

To turn on Google Signals, the user should start in the GA4 admin menu, then choose Data Settings, and then Data Collection as shown below.

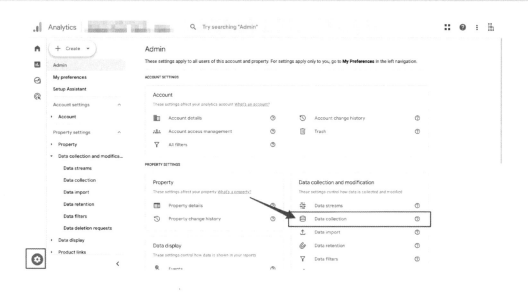

Once a user chooses the Data Collection submenu, they will come to the next screen. To turn on Google Signals, the user should simply slide the switch on as shown in the screenshot. Users should also turn off the setting for including Google Signals data in reporting identity. This combination of settings will limit data thresholding, which is detailed later in the book.

Event Retention:

In the GA4 admin menu, the user should choose Data Settings and then Data Retention as shown below:

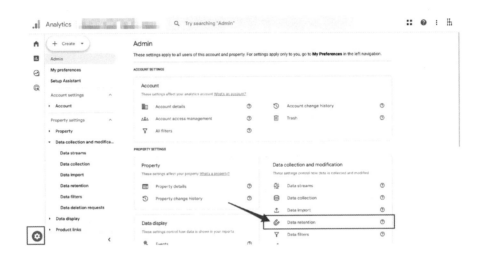

Once the user chooses the Data Retention submenu, they will come to the next screen. This setting is for how long GA4 will retain event data for reporting in Explorations. The default is two months, but we recommend extending it for up to fourteen months. That will allow a user to track more past events in Explorations, especially ones that were not created from GA4 conversions. There will be more on creating conversions later on.

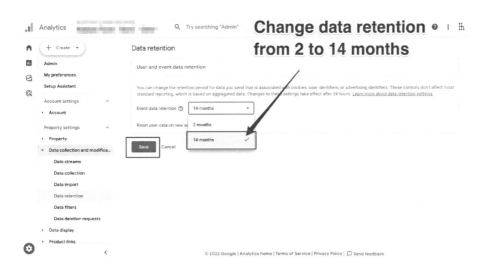

Ignore Duplicate Tags:

In the GA4 admin menu, the user should choose Data Streams and then click on their individual stream:

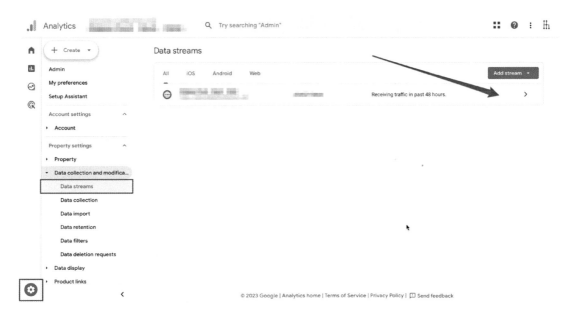

Once a user clicks on their data stream, they are taken to the following screen:

The user should then scroll down on the page and select Configure tag settings as shown above.

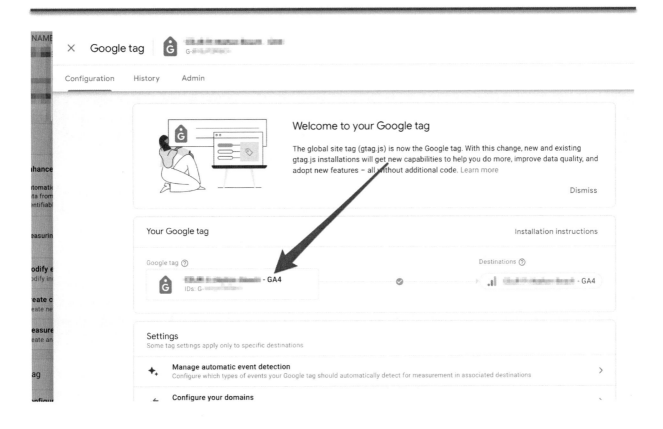

From the configure tag screen, the user should click on the Google tag, as shown above.

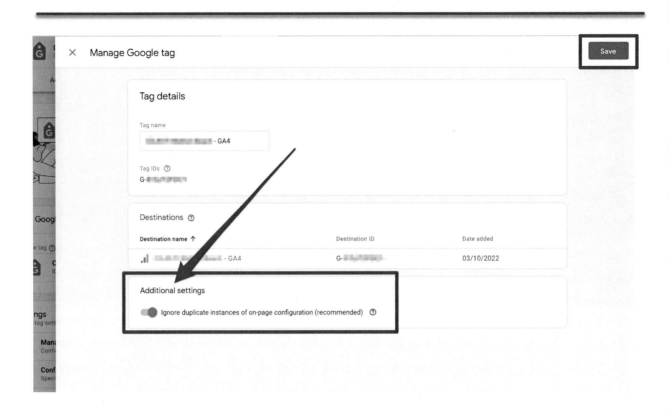

After clicking on the Google tag, the user is taken to the above screen. They should turn on the setting to "Ignore duplicate instances of on-page configuration" and that will prevent duplicate tags from potentially firing.

Placing GA4 Code on a Dealer Website

The last step in the setup process is to take the new GA4 Stream Name and the new GA4 Measurement ID and send both of them to the dealership's website provider. From the admin menu in GA4, the user should select their data stream as shown below:

Once the Data Stream is selected, the user is taken to the next screen.

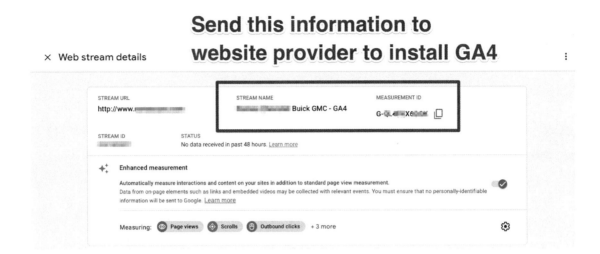

Send this information to website provider to install GA4

The dealership should copy both the stream name and the Measurement ID and email them to their website provider. The Measurement ID is the most important. It always starts with a G- and functions like a social security number for each GA4 property.

Here is a sample email a dealer could send to their website provider in order to get the new GA4 code live on their site:

Attn Website Support:

We need your help for installing Google Analytics 4 (GA4) code onto the www.yourdealerwebsite.com website.

Here is the GA4 Stream Name and Measurement ID:

https://www.yourdealewebsite.com – GA4

G-NQTXNKTZ93

Please let us know when the stream is live. Thank you for your help!

George Nenni

Connecting Google Ads with GA4

Once the new GA4 code is live on the website, the next step is to get the dealership's Google Ads account connected with GA4.

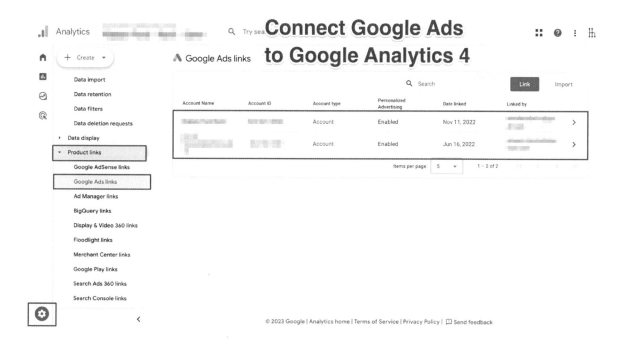

As a reminder, Google Ads is the software platform the dealer's agency is using to purchase Google paid search keywords. Google Ads contains the paid keywords, the consumer search queries, cost-per-click (CPC), as well as many other important data fields. We want this powerful data incorporated into GA4.

By connecting the dealership's Google Ads to their new GA4 installation, dealers gain full transparency with agency performance. In addition, they also unlock insights into how car shoppers are engaging with their advertising, how shoppers initially visit their website, and finally how they complete the various goals or conversions on the dealership website.

The process is simple but, before beginning, a dealer must first have the following permission levels:

1. In GA4, the dealer must have an Editor role for the property they wish to link.
2. The dealership needs administrative access in Google Ads.

A user simply clicks on the admin menu in GA4 which is the small gear icon in the lower left corner. They should then click on the link in the middle column for Google Ads Links. Once they click that, the user needs to locate the Google Ads account they wish to be connected with the new GA4.

GOOGLE ANALYTICS EVENTS

What are They and Why are They Important?

Since Google Analytics 4 is based 100 percent around events, let's dive deeper into events and how they change for GA4. A Google Analytics event is a trigger that fires and it allows users to measure website interactions such as loading a page, scrolling down a page, clicking a link, chat messaging, or lead form generation.

Events are important as they allow a user to customize the GA4 reporting by tracking the most important events. That is accomplished by selecting certain GA4 events to also be counted as conversions. We will discuss conversions later in this book, but they are the same as Goals in Google Analytics Universal. In Universal, goals could be created through page views and other methods. In GA4, goals are now called conversions, and they must come from an associated event.

Automotive Standards Council (ASC)

Within the automotive industry, the Automotive Standards Council for GA4 (ASC) was formed by Brian Pasch in order to create common guidelines for the transition to Google Analytics 4. The standards will include commonly-named events designed to accommodate the needs of automotive, RV, marine, and powersports dealers. In November 2022, the Council released the first version (1.0) of the specifications.

The commonly-named events all begin with the prefix of asc such as asc_click-to-call or asc_form_submission. These standards not only allow GA4 users to more easily identify key events to mark as conversions, but they also allow for consistency across website and third-party website tool vendors. One of the biggest benefits for car dealers, if they switch website toll providers such as messaging or trade, is that there is virtually zero work involved to change the GA4 conversions tracking.

The ASC specification also includes over fifty parameters that live within the asc events. These parameters are part of the amazing new power of GA4 because they can carry additional information that can be passed through with the conversion. GA4 users can have up to twenty-five parameters for each event. Event parameter names can have up to forty characters while the individual values assigned to each parameter must be a hundred characters or less. Virtually any information from the vehicle detail page (VDP) — including vehicle year, make, model, VIN, stock number, and even the first-seen date of the vehicle — can be passed through events as parameters. How might this improve dealership reporting in GA4? An example is that instead of reporting on lead forms by channel, a dealership could break it out between new versus used versus certified or vehicles older than sixty days versus younger than fifteen days.

In order to report on the new GA4 event parameters, the user needs to create custom dimensions for each of the parameters. Not all of the fifty ASC parameters will typically be used. The council suggests creating thirty-four custom dimensions to align with the thirty-four parameters deemed valuable for GA4 reports. If dealers do not create custom dimensions for each of the thirty-four parameters suggested by ASC, that will limit their ability to generate insightful GA4 reports.

Note: For dealers using website providers, Dealer eProcess or Dealer Inspire, those thirty-four parameters should already have been created by their support teams, and the dealers should verify that.

As of the printing of this book, here is a list of the thirty-four parameters for which ASC recommends dealers create custom dimensions:

- affiliation
- comm_outcome
- comm_status
- comm_type

- currency
- department
- element_text
- element_type
- element_value
- event_action
- event_action_result
- event_owner
- flow_name
- flow_outcome
- form_name
- form_type
- item_category
- item_color
- item_condition
- item_fuel_type
- item_id
- item_inventory_date
- item_make
- item_model
- item_number
- item_payment
- item_price
- item_type
- item_variant
- item_year
- media_type
- page_location
- page_type
- product_name
- promotion_name

Note: You'll notice the list above has thirty-five entries. We think item_inventory_date is an important parameter to create a custom dimension for. This allows reporting on aging inventory compared to website and conversion activity.

Currently, more and more automotive website and tool providers are rolling out their ASC events. We applaud these efforts as it makes life easier for dealers, agencies, and vendors. More details can be found on the ASC website: **www.automotivestandardscouncil.com**

On the next page is a look at some default and custom events in a GA4 property. Users can check their own events by going to the Admin menu on the left and then choosing the Events menu option.

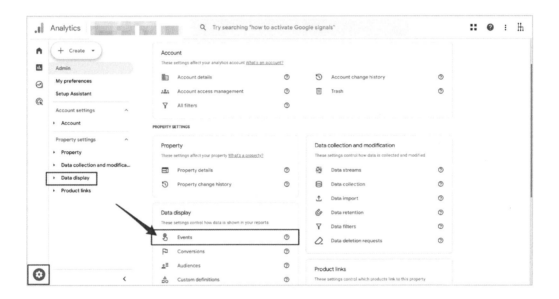

There are three primary types of events in GA4, and here is how they break down:

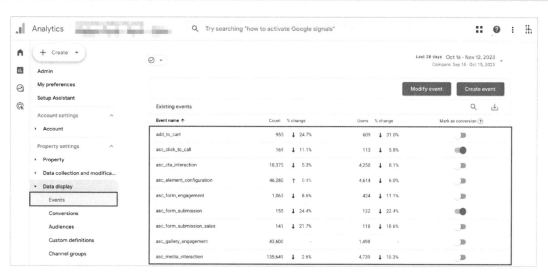

1. **Automatic Events:** After dealers add the Google Analytics 4 tracking code to their website, the system will automatically track a number of events when someone views a page. The following events are tracked automatically and cannot be turned off:

   a) The page view event shows the website page the user is viewing.

   b) The first visit event is triggered automatically the first time a visitor comes to the dealer website. This event is used to calculate New Users in the GA4 reporting.

   c) The user engagement event is fired and used to track visitors who spend at least ten seconds on the dealer website.

   d) The session start event tracks when a user session starts. A new session start event is triggered when a user has been inactive for at least thirty minutes

2. **Enhanced Measurement Events:** The following events are part of the Enhanced Measurement feature that automatically collects additional data. With the Enhanced Measurement events, users can turn them on or off as they prefer:

   a) Scroll: Reporting on visitors scrolling at least 90 percent of a page.

   b) Click: Outbound clicks from the dealer's website.

   c) Form interactions: Capturing shopper interactions with lead forms.

   d) Video start, video progress, and video complete: Metrics showing shoppers who are viewing website-embedded YouTube videos.

   e) File download: Reporting on shoppers downloading content from the dealer website.

3. **Custom Events:** These events can be created in GA4 or within Google Tag Manager. As automotive website and digital retailing tool providers upgrade their Universal events to GA4 events, they will flow through as custom events. Some custom events can be simply marked as a conversion-event, but others need to be further customized using parameters within GA4 (more on creating custom events later). We feel custom events are a key differentiation point for automotive website and plug-in tool providers because of the degree to which they pass key website information to the custom event by using parameters. We hope to see more automotive website and tool companies rolling out their ASC events because that will help to simplify GA4 setup and make measurement more consistent.

ASC EVENTS

What are They and How to Implement Them?

As mentioned earlier, the Automotive Standards Council (ASC) for Google Analytics 4 was formed by Brian Pasch in the automotive industry in order to create common guidelines for the transition to Google Analytics 4. These standards will include commonly-named events designed to accommodate the needs of automotive retailers.

The challenge for many dealers is that while the ASC guidelines specify the naming conventions for events and parameters, they don't explain how to implement them in GA4. We will explain how the ASC events work, and then we'll walk users through a few examples for a more hands-on explanation.

From a high-level discussion, there will be events to mark as a conversion (lead forms, phone calls, etc.), and there will be events that are interesting but should not be marked as conversions (vehicle detail page views, form engagement, etc.). We will show users how to treat GA4 events for both of these scenarios.

For the events that will be marked as conversion-events in GA4, there are two types of ASC conversion events:

1. **Simple ASC conversion events:** These are ASC events we wish to mark as a conversion, and the only work required is to do so. Examples of simple ASC events are website lead forms and website mobile click to calls. Both of these ASC events can be simply marked in blue as conversions, as shown below:

2. **Complex ASC conversion events:** These are ASC events that have underlying parameters that users need to reference in order to create custom ASC events. Any parameters that users wish to reference and report on need to have custom dimensions created for them. Examples of complex events requiring parameter referencing would be ASC events from third-party website plug-in tools such as messaging, digital retailing, or trade tools.

REQUESTING ASC EVENT FIRING

Measurement IDs and API Secrets

Whether dealers are setting up simple ASC events or complex ASC events, they will need the help of their automotive website vendors and third-party website tool providers.

When requesting ASC events, a technology vendor may ask for one or both of the following elements:

Measurement ID

As discussed earlier, each GA4 property will have their own unique Measurement ID. This ID will always start with the prefix of G followed by a 10-digit alphanumeric string.

To locate the Measurement ID, the user should go to the admin menu and click on Data Streams as shown on the next page.

Once the user is on the Data Stream screen, they should click to select their website Data Stream. After choosing the Data Stream, the user is taken to the screen on the next page. They should simply click on the copy icon in order to copy the Measurement ID to their clipboard.

API Secret

The complex-sounding code is actually pretty simple. It is a secret code that dealers give to their vendors which prevents unauthorized parties from sending event data into a dealership's GA4 property. While automotive website providers usually do not need API secrets, third-party website tool providers often must utilize them.

To locate the API Secret, the user should stay on the same screen as shown earlier for the Measurement ID. Then they should scroll to the bottom and select Measurement Protocols and API secrets as shown on the next page.

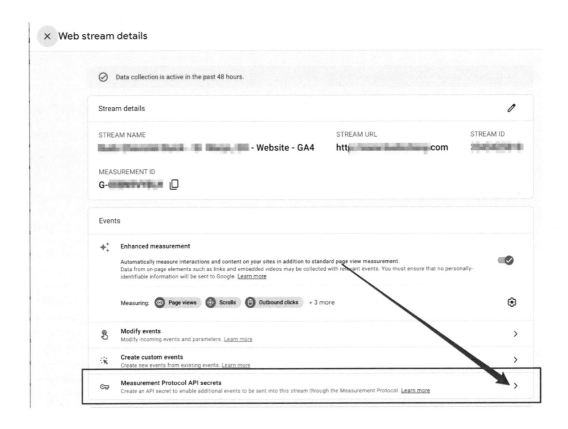

After selecting Measurement Protocols and API secrets, the user is taken to the next screen.

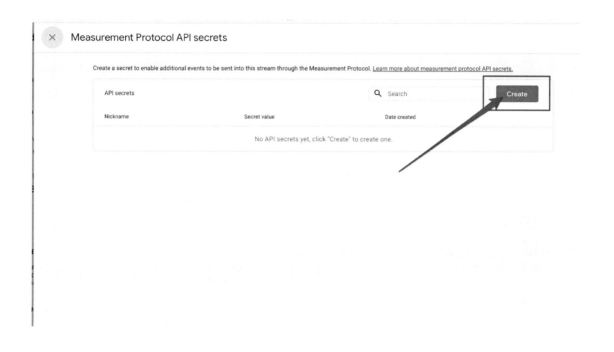

In the above screen, the user can see a list of any existing API secrets. Users should remember that each third-party website tool provider needs to have their own API secret code. This allows dealers to turn off cancelled providers so they no longer have access to GA4 data. From the above screen, the user should click on the Create button to build a new API secret.

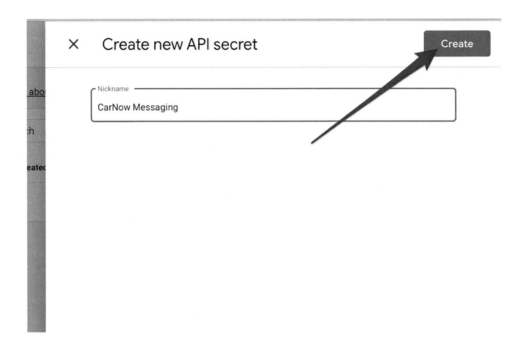

Once the user clicks to create a new API secret, they are taken to the screen above. They simply create a nickname for the API secret, choosing a name that identifies the vendor. In our example, we are building an API secret that we will email to CarNow's support team to get GA4 events firing. After entering the nickname, the user should click the Create button.

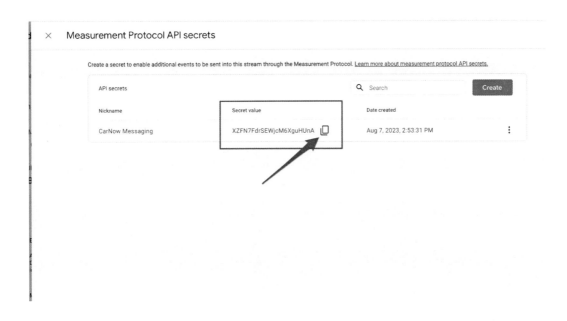

After creating the new API secret, it should appear in a list as shown above. The user can simply click the copy icon, copy the new API secret to their clipboard, and then send this information to the appropriate support team.

ASC CUSTOM EVENT EXAMPLES

We will walk readers through a few custom ASC GA4 examples for events that users may want to mark as conversions and for events users may simply want to track but not include in conversions. Once users become comfortable with the process, they can apply this same approach in GA4 to other third-party tool complex events. Overall, the process is similar, and follows this workflow:

1. Create a custom GA4 event, referencing parameters within existing ASC events.
2. Create a custom dimension for each parameter that is referenced in step 1. Website providers such as Dealer eProcess and Dealer Inspire provide this step as a customer courtesy.
3. Wait for new custom events to fire in GA4, and then mark them as conversions if desired.

Example 1: Custom ASC Events for CarNow Messaging Starts

CarNow is just one example of an automotive messaging provider that follows the ASC event standards. Automotive messaging tools fire events with the prefix of asc_comm, and here are two examples:

asc_comm_engagement: An event is fired in GA4 whenever a consumer interacts with a chat or SMS platform. Every chat or text response from a consumer will fire this event, so, clearly, this is more than a dealership would measure. Instead, the dealer only wants to track a subset of the asc_comm_engagement events.

asc_comm_submission: An event is fired when a chat or SMS session gathers consumer information that will flow to the dealership's CRM.

Note: This is a good example of a simple ASC conversion event that can be simply marked as a conversion without creating a custom event as shown below:

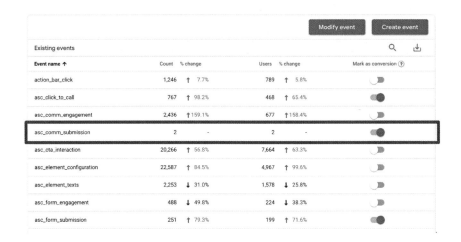

In order to build a new metric for measuring the unique number of chats, the user needs to reference an underlying parameter within the **asc_comm_engagement** GA4 event.

Note: Automotive GA4 users should not simply mark the **asc_comm_engagement** event as a conversion since that would measure every single chat communication and would overstate the chat conversions by far. Instead, the dealership is more interested in tracking a subset of the **asc_comm_engagement** events. There are three steps for that:

1. Create a new event in GA4 named **asc_chat_started** that references the underlying parameter **comm_status** in the existing **asc_comm_engagement** events.
2. Create a custom dimension for the event parameter **comm_status** so that the user can pull out the event parameter value of **start**.
3. Wait for the new custom event, **asc_chat_started,** to fire in GA4, and then mark it as a conversion event.

In the first step, a new event in GA4 is created that references the underlying parameter in an existing event. From the admin menu, the user should go to the Events submenu and then click the button for Create Event.

After the user chooses the Create events menu item, they should then select the Create button.

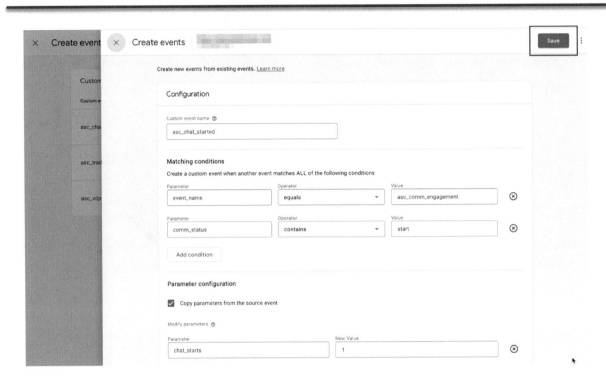

The user should fill in the configuration as shown in the screen above. The process flow is to create a new event called **asc_chat_started** that will reference the original event of **asc_comm_engagement** while, at the same time, referencing an existing event parameter named **comm_status** and referencing the event parameter value of **start**.

Note: The actual GA4 event the user will eventually use is the custom event named **asc_chat_started**. When the user has completed the process, they will slide this event over to mark it as a conversion event.

The next step is for the user to create a custom dimension for the event parameter named **comm_status** so that they can reference the parameter value of **start**. In GA4, you can set up fifty event-scoped custom dimensions.

As mentioned earlier, custom dimensions allow users to reference the many powerful underlying parameters within the new ASC events. Many dealers are proactively creating custom dimensions for each of the thirty-four parameters suggested by ASC.

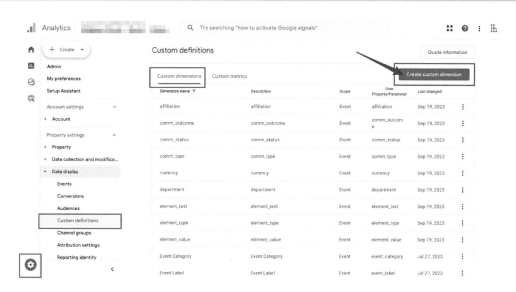

Note: For dealers using website providers, Dealer eProcess or Dealer Inspire, those thirty-four parameters should already be created by their support teams although the dealers should verify that.

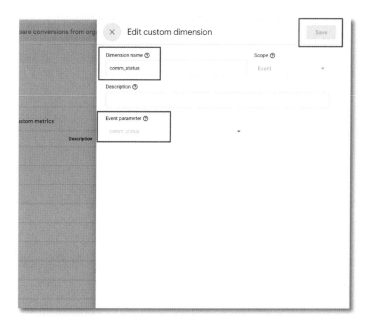

Once the setup is complete and within twenty-four hours or so, users will see a new custom event named **asc_chat_started** listed in the GA4 events, and they can slide that over to mark it as a conversion event as shown on the next page.

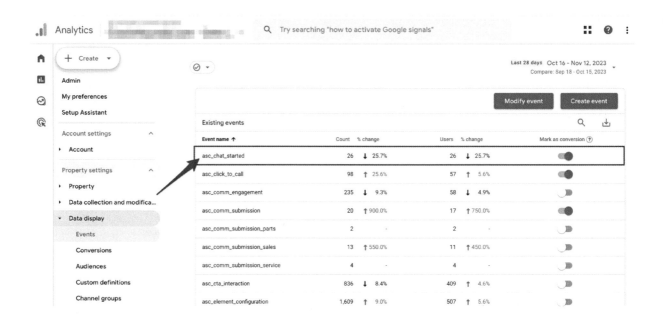

Example 2: Custom ASC Events for TradePending Trade Tool Leads

TradePending is just one example of an automotive trade tool provider that follows the ASC event standards. Dealers should track automotive trade tools with the event, **asc_form_submission**, while referencing a **department** parameter having a value of **trade**.

TradePending fires asc form events in GA4 and, currently, there is no standard event for tracking trade leads although we are requesting that from ASC. Therefore, users must build a new custom event for trade leads by referencing the underlying department parameter within the **asc_form_submission** GA4 event. There are three steps:

1. Create a new event in GA4 named **asc_trade_leads** that references the underlying parameter **department** in the existing **asc_form_submission** event.
2. Create a custom dimension for the existing event parameter **department** so that we can pull out the existing event parameter value of **trade**.
3. Wait for new custom event **asc_trade_leads** to fire in GA4, and then mark them as conversion events.

In the first step, a new event is created and named **asc_trade_leads** in GA4, and it references the underlying parameter **department** in the existing event **asc_form_submission**.

From the admin menu, the user should go to Events and then click the button for Create Event.

Once the user chooses the Create events menu, they should select Create.

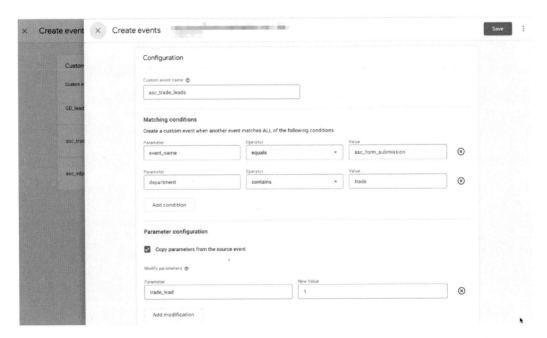

The user should fill in the configuration as shown in the screen above. They will be creating a new event called **asc_trade_leads** that will reference the original event of **asc_form_submission**. The existing event parameter named **department** will be called out, and the existing event parameter value of **trade** will be referenced.

Note: The actual GA4 event that will eventually be used is the custom event named **asc_trade_leads**. When the process is completed, the user will slide this event over to mark it as a conversion event.

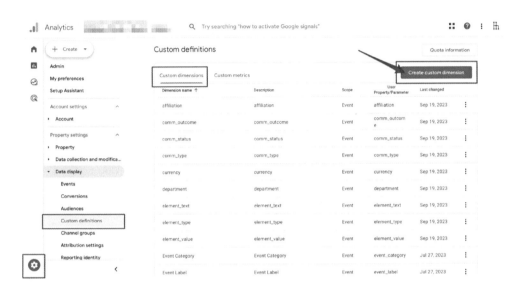

The next step is for the user to create a custom dimension for the event parameter named **department** so that they can reference the parameter value of **trade**.

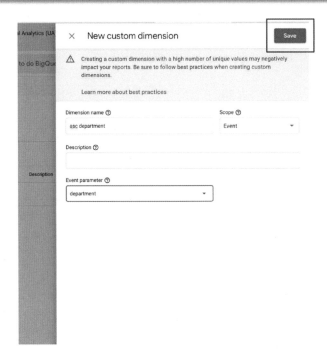

Once the setup is complete and within twenty-four hours or so, users will see this new custom event named **asc_trade_leads** listed in the GA4 events, and they can slide it over to mark it as a conversion event.

Managing Data Thresholding in GA4

As mentioned earlier, if users find that some events or traffic is missing from their GA4 reports, that could be due to Google Analytics applying a data threshold. These thresholds are used to protect the privacy of individual users by preventing the supposition of their identities through demographics, interests, or other signals in the data.

If a dealership website has few users during a specific range of dates, and Google Signals is on, some data in reports or explorations may not be shown.

When a user views a report or exploration with a narrow date range and very few sessions or events are appearing, it could be that GA4 data thresholds might be applied and that they hide some information. To see the hidden data, the user needs to try expanding the date range which could reveal more triggering events.

If expanding the date range doesn't solve the data thresholding issue, the next step is for the user to change the Reporting Identity in order to try and get the hidden data to appear. The process is simple. The user first goes to the admin menu in GA4 and then clicks on Reporting Identity in the middle column as shown on the next page.

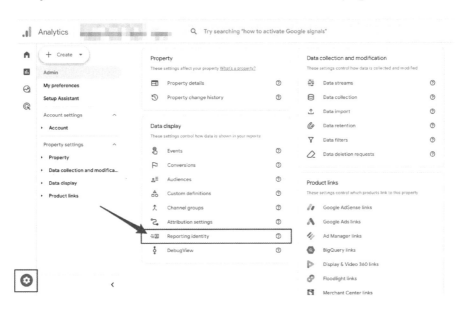

Once the user clicks on Reporting Identity, they will be taken to the following screen. The user should click on Show all, to expand the menu.

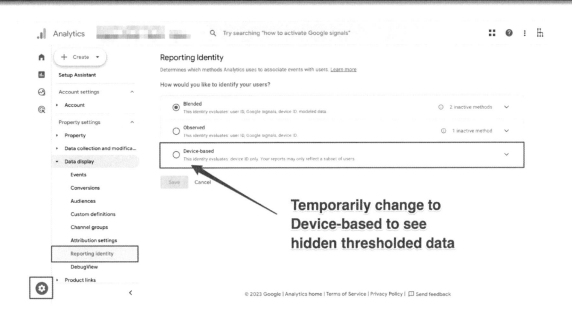

Once the user has expanded the menu, they should see that the current selection is Blended. The user should change that to Device-based, approve the disclaimer question, and then click save. This is a temporary switch, and users will want to switch back after this testing is complete.

Once the user switches to Device-based, they should then check for any missing GA4 events or traffic sources. After switching to Device-based and users still do not see missing events or traffic, then they should continue troubleshooting with their agency, website, or plug-in tool providers.

MENUS AND NAVIGATION

Home

When a user first navigates to a Google Analytics 4 property, they will land on the home screen as shown below:

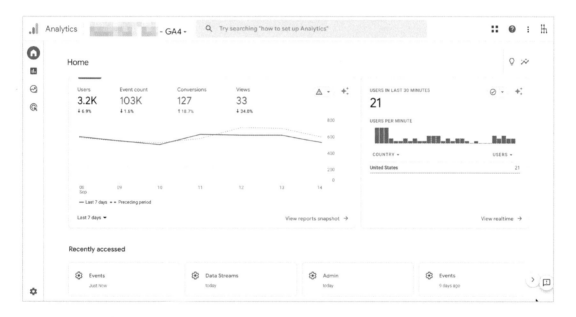

The home screen in GA4 provides a top-down overview of a dealership's website performance. The home screen shows high-level traffic and engagement metrics with quick links for drilling down.

On the right-hand side there is a link to inspect website analytics in real time, showing shoppers and activities that are currently occurring on the dealer website.

A helpful new feature of GA4 is that the home screen now shows the most recently viewed pages. That can be very helpful for finding reports that were recently viewed.

Reports

The Reports menu in GA4 contains the most out-of-the-box reporting and menu options for the user. There are reports on traffic, engagement, conversions, retention, and more. For most users, the Reports menu will handle most of the reporting needs for the dealership.

For richer reporting, the GA4 user would need to utilize the Explore menu, and we will cover that in a later section.

Above are a few of the most popular tools dealers should experiment with inside the Reports menu. The most commonly used tools include:

- **Add comparison:** Similar to adding traffic segments in Universal Analytics, it allows the user to add traffic comparisons. For instance, the dealer may want to compare organic search traffic with paid search traffic.

- **Change date range:** The user can either choose from pre-selected date ranges or choose a custom range for reporting.
- **Share:** Allows the dealer to create a shareable link to a report or to download to a PDF or CSV file (comma separated value for importing to Excel).
- **Customize:** Allows the user to customize the cards that display for each report. Cards can be added, removed, or repositioned.

Reports Snapshot

The Reports Snapshot is the perfect place for users to start their reporting journey in GA4. That summary screen shows similar information as the Home screen, but it also adds traffic sources, geographic locations, pages viewed, events triggered, as well as conversions.

Any of those summary areas can be drilled down in to instantly move into deeper reporting options within the GA4 menus.

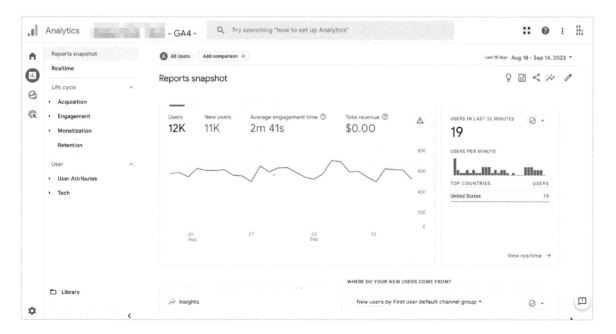

Realtime

The Realtime reports can be accessed either through the GA4 menus or by drilling down from either the home page or the Reports Snapshot page. Those reports allow the dealer to monitor activity on their website as it occurs. The various cards in this reporting view allows the user to see how shoppers are first arriving on the website, how they are moving through the conversion funnel, and how they are engaging with the dealer website.

The Realtime reports include:

- Users during the last thirty minutes
- Users by first source
- Users by page
- Event names, event counts, event parameters, and parameter values
- Conversion types and counts

Parameter Inspection

One of the most useful elements of the Realtime overview report is the ability to monitor events and parameters. As of the writing of this book, the Realtime reports are also the only location in GA4 where the user can inspect parameters that are firing within events. Inspecting these parameters can be very helpful when building custom events and determining which parameters should be referenced for which parameter values.

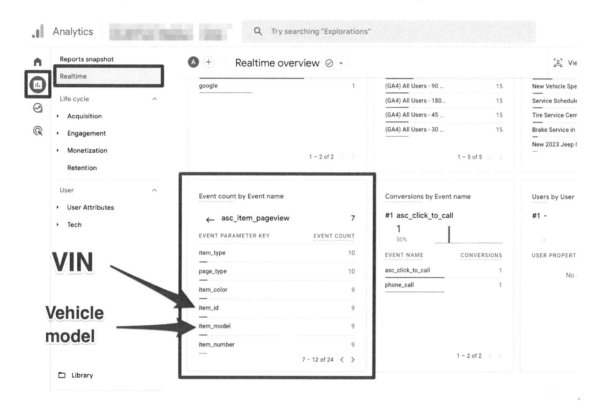

Above is an example of viewing ASC event parameters in the GA4 Realtime overview report. Once the user clicks on the event for **asc_item_pageview**, they can view the various event parameters such **item_id** (vehicle VIN) or **item_model** (vehicle model). The ability to pass event parameters into reporting is one of the amazing elements of GA4. For example, instead of reporting on lead forms from a paid search, the user could break that out by vehicle make, model, year, etc.

Life Cycle

Acquisition

Acquisition overview: The Acquisition reports in GA4 help the dealer to better understand where new and returning users are coming from. For example, dealerships can use the reports to see how many users found their website using paid Facebook ads.

The first choice in the Acquisition menu is the Acquisition Overview. This report summarizes the dealership's acquisition data to help inspect the source and quality of their website traffic. Dealers can customize the individual cards in the report.

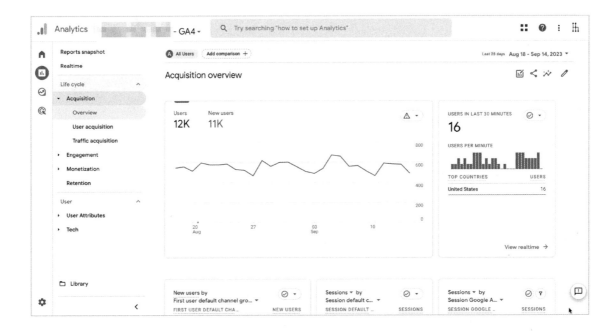

User acquisition: The User Acquisition reports in GA4 help dealers to see how they first acquired the users who were active in the selected date range. For example, suppose the dealership acquired a user in March 2022 but inspected the report for July 2022. If the user was active in July 2022, then the dealership would see how they first acquired that user in March 2022.

Another way to think about User Acquisition reports is that they are based on first-click attribution. That means that once the source, medium, and campaign are established when the user first visits the website, those UTM parameters will never change.

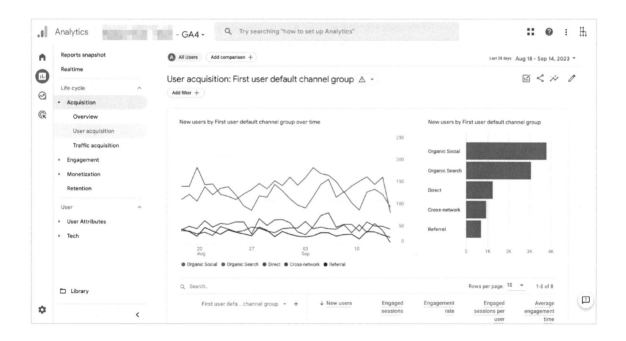

The First user default channel grouping is the default dimension but, as seen in the screenshot below, the user can change dimensions.

Note: All of the dimension choices start with the prefix of **first user**.

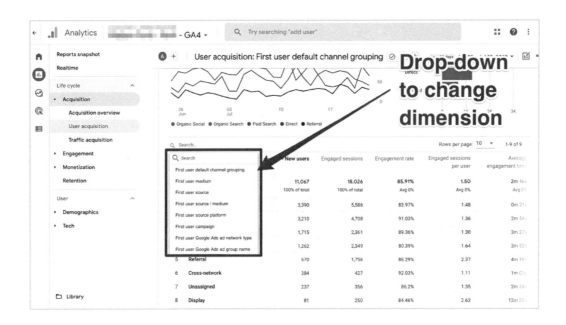

Traffic acquisition: While the User acquisition report shows data on the first visit, the Traffic acquisition report shows dealers the data about sessions from both new and returning users.

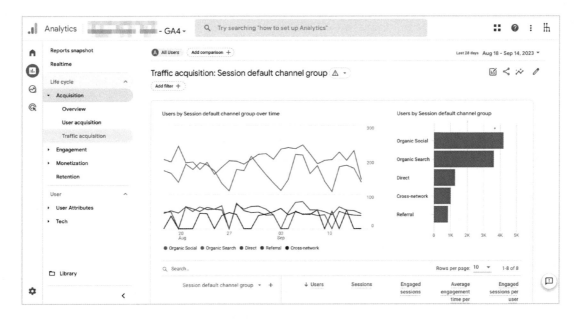

The default dimension for the Traffic acquisition menu is session default channel grouping. The user can change dimensions as seen in screenshot below.

Another way to think about Traffic Acquisition reports is that they are based on last-click attribution. That means that the source, medium, and campaign for any conversion events will be determined during the final website visit.

Note: All of the dimension choices start with the prefix of **session**.

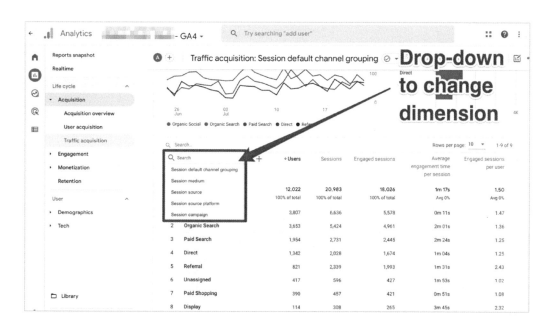

Engagement

Engagement overview: The Engagement reports in GA4 allow the dealer to measure user engagement by the events and conversion events that users trigger. The reports can help dealers see where website visitors are engaging and converting.

Any of the individual cards can be drilled down to inspect individual events, pages, retention, and more.

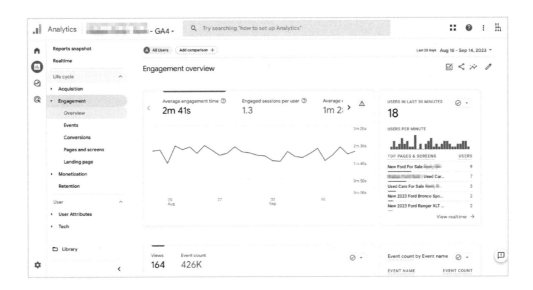

Events: The Events submenu in the Engagement menu allows the dealer to inspect events over time, as well as individual metrics around each event. The dealer can then click on any event to drill down to more granular metrics.

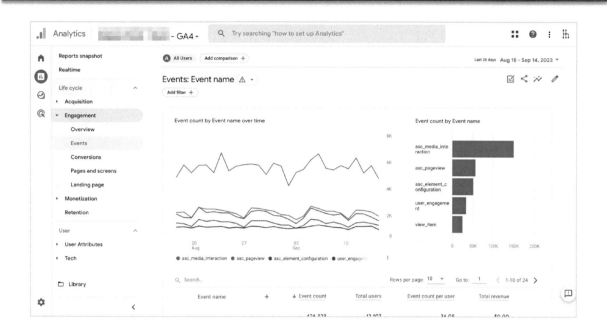

Conversions: The Conversions submenu in the Engagement menu allows the dealer to inspect conversions over time as well as individual metrics around each conversion.

The dealer can then click on any conversion to drill down to more granular metrics.

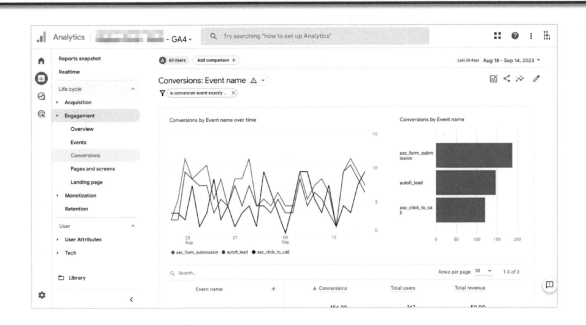

Pages and screens: The Pages and screens submenu in the Engagement menu allows the dealer to see the website pages by adding information about them to events. As we mentioned previously, everything in GA4 is measured around events. Dealers can generate reports showing the top pages that their shoppers are engaging with.

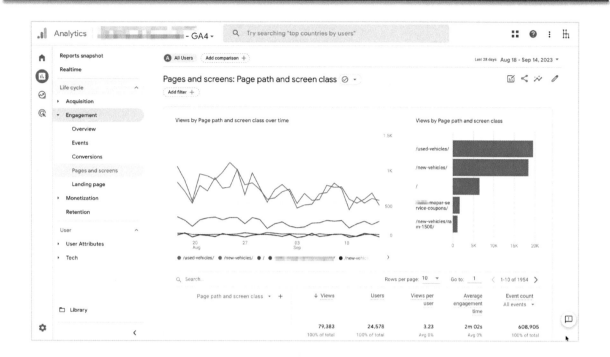

Landing page: The Landing page submenu in the Engagement menu allows the dealer to easily inspect the landing pages for the website. By filtering these landing pages by source or campaign, the user can drill deeper. For instance, often a dealership will pay for search engine optimization (SEO) and the provider will build SEO content landing pages designed to rank high in Google search. By filtering the landing pages by the organic search channel, the user can measure how well these SEO landing pages are performing.

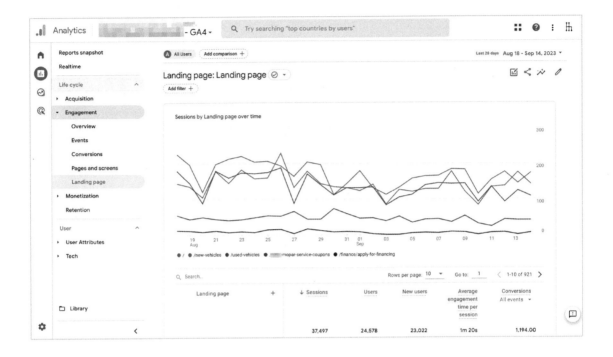

Monetization

The Monetization reporting in GA4 is geared more toward true e-commerce versus traditional dealership digital marketing.

As dealers are doing fewer online transactions but more online-assisted transactions and brick-and-mortar transactions, the Monetization menu will not be a part of today's regular reporting. As advances are made with automotive e-commerce, we look forward to making better use of the monetization reporting in GA4.

Retention

The Retention report helps dealerships inspect how often and for how long users engage with their website after their first visit.

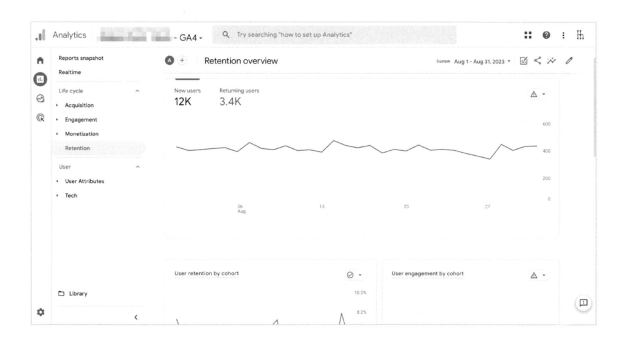

User

Demographics

Demographics overview: The Demographics reports help dealers break out their users by location, language, gender, and interests. As with most GA4 reports, they include interactive charts, diagrams, and tables with drill-down capability to help dealers better visualize the data.

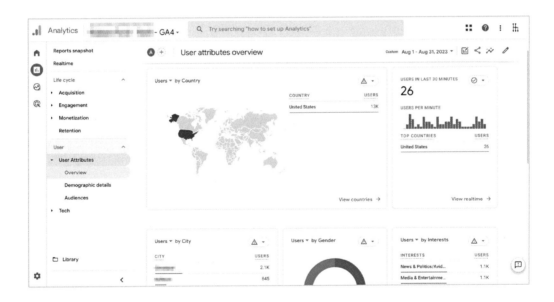

Demographics details: The Demographics Details reports goes into a deeper level of reporting compared to the Demographics overview, including a table showing traffic and engagement metrics broken out by country.

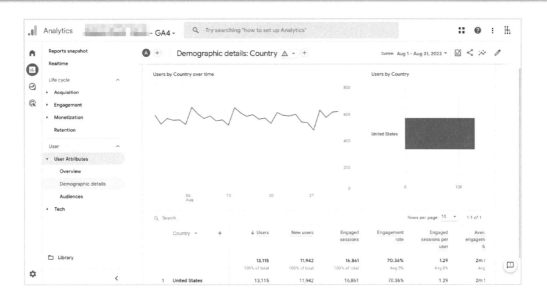

Tech

Tech overview: The Tech reports show traffic broken down by the technology used. Technology elements include mobile versus desktop, browsers, and operating systems as well as screen resolution. The overview gives the dealer a number of relevant cards they can view and drill down on.

The data can be useful for making sure the dealership is getting their fair share of mobile traffic, or they can look for strange technology patterns that could indicate bot traffic.

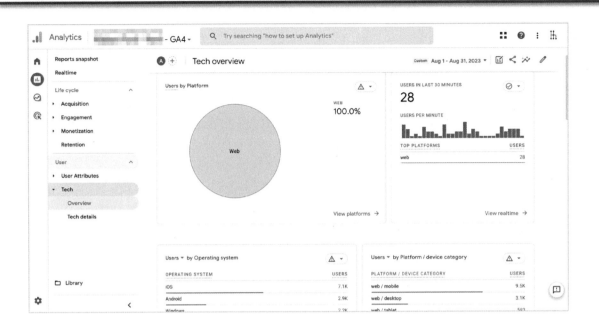

Tech details: The Tech details report goes a level deeper, showing trending data and amplification reports as well as tables. As with many detail reports, this report can be customized by the dealer.

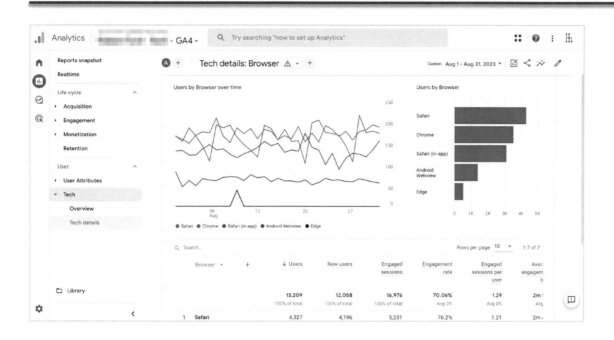

Library

The Library in GA4 is a central location to house reports or collections of reports. A dealer can customize all of the reports or copy them in addition to creating them.

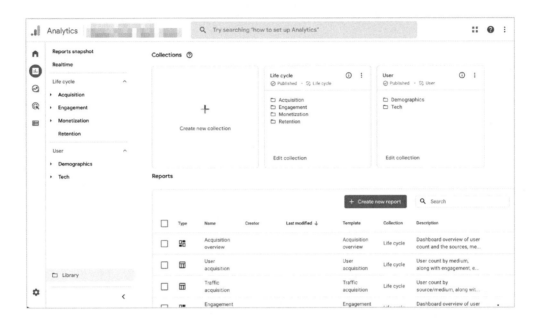

All of the collections and reports are organized in one place where a dealer can customize them and create more of them. A collection is simply a group of reports, and dealers can create and organize their own collections. There are two default collections already created, one for Lifecycle reports and one for User reports.

Collections

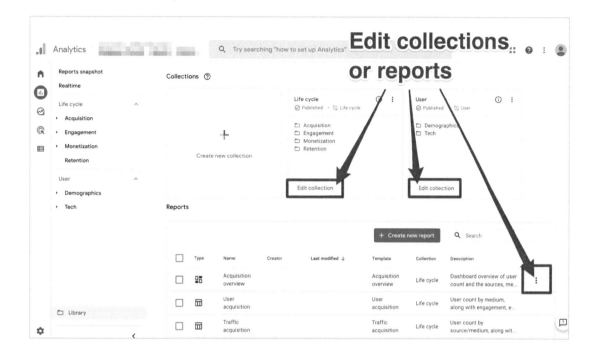

As mentioned, collections are groups of reports that can be customized within the Library. In the screenshot above, the user is customizing one of the default collections, the Life Cycle collection. By dragging and dropping, the user can customize which reports are included in each collection.

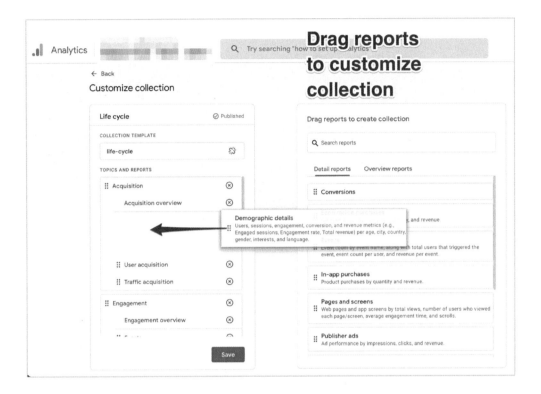

Reports

Existing default reports can be edited and customized within the Library, but the user must have editor access in GA4. Users can also create brand-new reports within the Library from scratch. There is a maximum of 200 custom reports allowed per GA4 property.

The next screenshot shows a user editing the Acquisition Overview report. The user simply adds new cards or deletes existing cards.

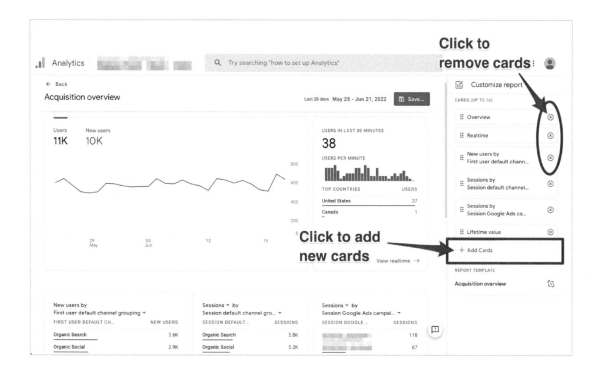

Explore

Explorations

Another menu opens up a powerful new GA4 reporting capability, and it is called Explorations under the Explore menu. It allows a dealer to go beyond standard GA4 reports with incredible flexibility, unlocking additional insights into website shopping behavior.

The standard GA4 reports are designed to inspect the key success metrics for a dealership. Explorations in GA4 allows nearly full customization, allowing segments and filters as well as deciding which dimensions and metrics are included.

As seen in the screenshot that follows, a user can either build an exploration from a template or create an entirely new exploration.

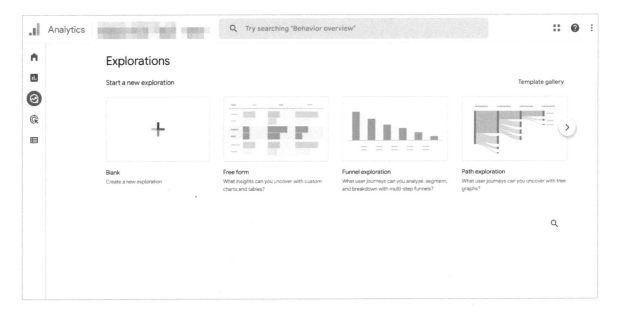

The explorations templates include:

- **Free form:** Allows the user to combine tables with various graphing elements like pie charts, line charts, and more
- **Funnel**: Analyzing and breaking down the shopping journey.
- **Path**: Similar to funnel but with a waterfall approach to visualization.
- **Segment Overlap**: Using a Venn diagram approach, helps the user visualize how user segments may overlap.
- **User**: Helps the analyst see how different user streams, such as web versus app, impact the shopping journey.
- **Cohort**: Shows the tendency for similar groups of users or cohorts to return to the website after first visits.

On the next page is an example of starting a new exploration using the free-form template. The column on the left contains the active variables that can be used in the exploration. Users can add or remove the available variables and then drag them from left to right into one or more tabs for active reports.

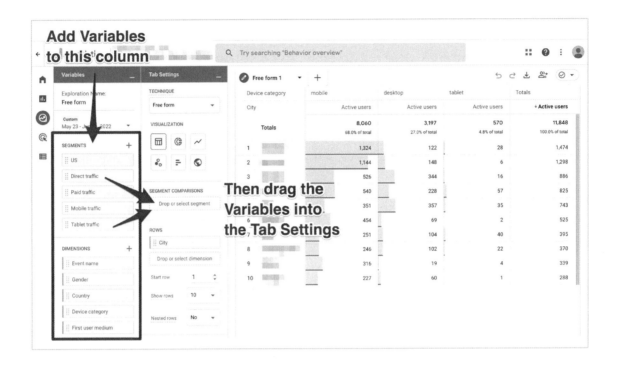

The area on the right-hand side of the page is called the canvas. The canvas will change as the user drags segments, dimensions, and metrics from left to right from the variables column into one or more of the tab settings.

Keep in mind that not every variable on the far-left column can be dragged into one of the tab settings. As you can see in the screenshot below, the dimensions must first go into the rows section. Then they can also be added to the columns section as a secondary dimension or even a tertiary dimension.

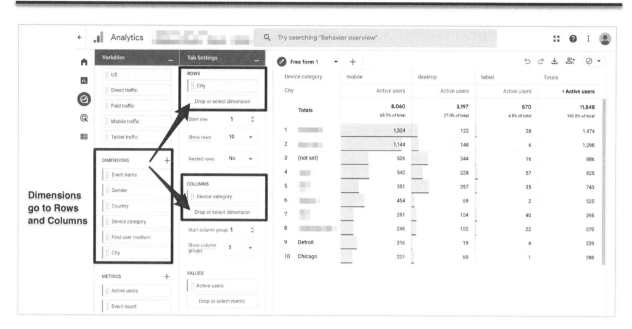

As shown in the next screenshot, the ability to add secondary and tertiary dimensions is one of the more powerful elements of the new GA4 reporting. Remember that the reports can sometimes come out in strange ways, depending on which dimensions are chosen.

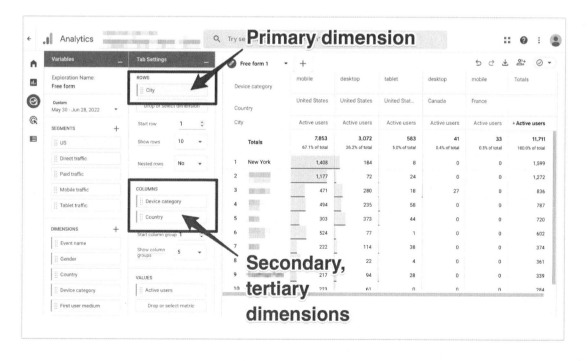

As mentioned earlier, not every variable on the far-left column can be dragged into one of the tab settings. As seen in the next screenshot, the metrics must go into the values section.

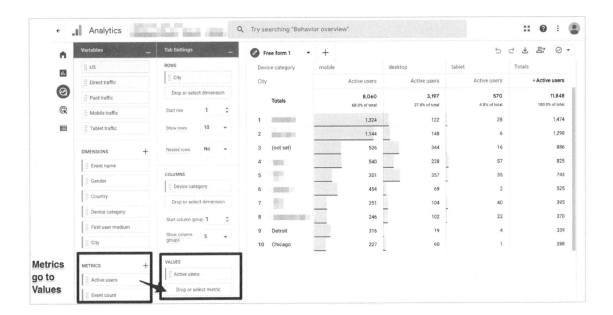

It is a little confusing as it would seem that the values are also landing in columns, but only dimensions go into columns. Here is a simple summary of how the user should frame this:

1. The primary dimension is the rows.
2. Slide other dimensions into the column section if you want to use secondary or tertiary dimensions.
3. Everything else—all of the metrics that will be listed in the columns—should go into the values section.

In the screenshot below is an example of an exploration report on Google paid search keywords purchased in the previous 30 days. This is a freeform report, with the only row being Session Google Ads keyword text. The values (which become columns) are:

- Google Ads clicks
- Google Ads cost per click
- Google Ads cost
- Sessions
- Engaged sessions
- Conversions

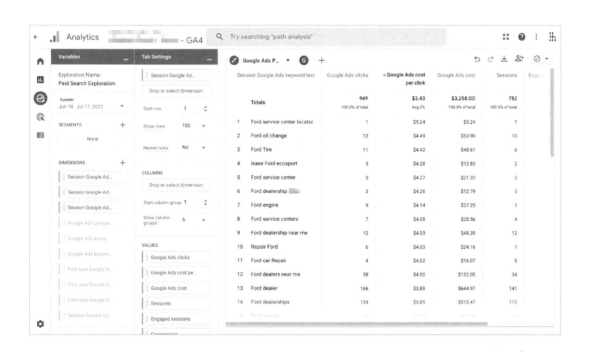

Practicing with explorations can also help the user become accustomed to some of the new GA4 metrics. A helpful breakdown of the new metrics and how they relate to one another is in the following screenshot.

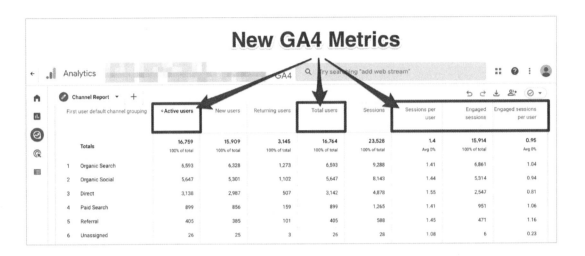

GA4 is a completely new approach to analytics, and it introduces a number of new metrics, including active users and engaged sessions. By practicing with explorations, dealers can become more comfortable with how these new metrics relate to one another.

A common mistake when building these new explorations is choosing the wrong dimensions, and that will not allow the new GA4 engagement metrics to be displayed. In the following screenshot, there is an example of selecting source/medium dimensions. There will be choices for Attribution and Traffic Source. The user should choose the dimensions under traffic source. They will start with the prefix of First user to indicate that the dimensions are about new users.

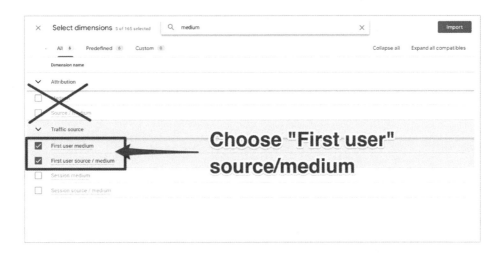

The reasoning behind these new metrics is based on the way GA4 is engineered, to look at users and their website sessions over time. In order to measure user engagement, the report first must categorize the users based on their first visit. The assumption is that the car shopping journey will involve several sessions to the website from that user. GA4 will measure the sessions and the engaged sessions over time that may or may not lead to a conversion. The Conversion Paths report in the following section on the Advertising menu provides reporting on the full website shopping journey.

When new explorations are built, they are only visible by the user who created the exploration. Users can share explorations with other property users who have viewer-level access. Those users will be able to view the reports, but they will not be able to edit them. That could be a helpful approach for allowing automotive vendors to have view access to common reports. The next screenshot shows the process for sharing a new exploration

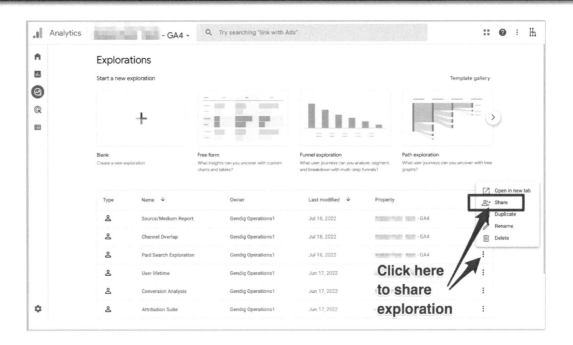

The user simply clicks the three dots (ellipsis) to open the menu and then clicks the Share button as shown in the following screenshot.

GA4 allows the creation of 200 explorations per user, per property. We recommend that dealers spend time in the exploration section of GA4, and that they experiment with different measurement dimensions and values.

Advertising

The Advertising menu in GA4 provides insight into the various shopping and conversion journeys occurring on dealership websites.

This section of GA4 could have been better named as Attribution for me because the reports break down and evaluate the various attribution models. Attribution is where we assign credit to various traffic sources that help the shopping journey along the way.

Advertising Snapshot

The Advertising Snapshot shown below gives a high-level overview of results. The user can then easily click on various areas for deeper dives.

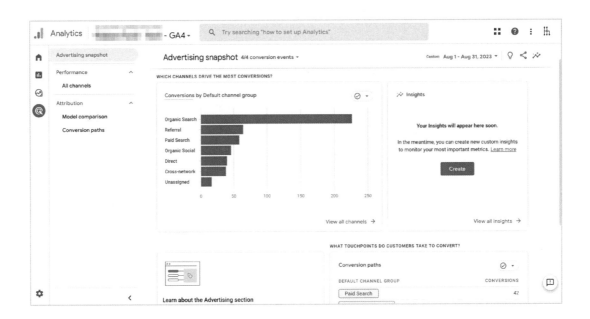

Attribution

Model comparison: This reporting section allows the user to compare how the various attribution models affect the conversion metrics. In the screenshot below, the user can click to drop down and compare the various attribution models.

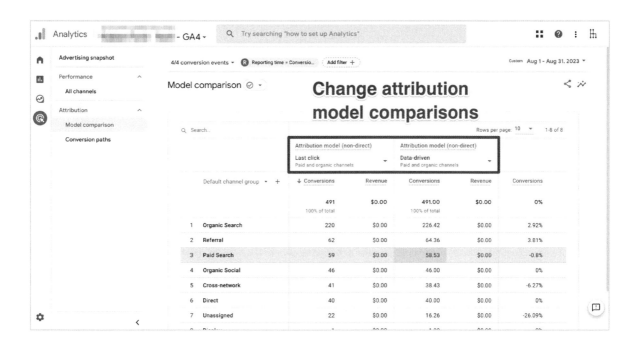

Here is a breakdown of the various attribution models in GA4:

1. **Cross Channel**
   - **Data-driven**: Conversion credit is based on the actual contribution for each conversion event for each channel or source/medium. This attribution model is unique in that it is custom for each dealer website.
   - **Last click**: A conversion credit of 100 percent is given to the last channel or source/medium that a shopper went through before converting.
   - **First click**: A conversion credit of 100 percent is given to the first channel or source/medium that a shopper went through before eventually converting.
   - **Linear**: Conversion credit is spread equally across all channels or source/mediums that a shopper went through before converting.

- **Position-based**: A conversion credit of 40 percent goes to both the first and last interactions, while the last 20 percent credit is distributed equally across the middle interactions of the shopping journey.
- **Time decay**: Conversion credit is given more to engagement points occurring closer to the actual conversion.

2. **Ads-preferred**

Last click: Conversion credit goes to the last Google Ads channel (paid search, display, YouTube, etc.) that a shopper went through before eventually converting. Only Google Ads channels are eligible for this conversion credit. For instance, if the shopper's path to conversion looked like this—Display > Social > Paid Search > Organic Search—then 100 percent of the conversion credit would go to Paid Search since it was the last paid Google channel in the shopping path.

Conversion paths: The Conversion paths report helps dealers learn more about the shopping journey from the first website visit, to subsequent return visits, and to eventual conversion. This tool also allows the dealer to understand a customer's paths to conversion and how different attribution models distribute credit on those paths.

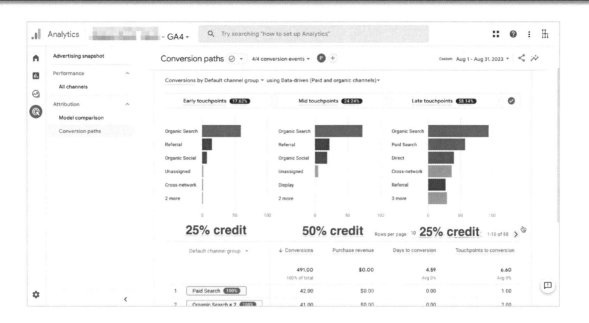

Above is a look at a Conversion paths report, showing the attribution credit being spread across three touchpoint buckets:

- **Early touchpoints**: During the shopping journey, the first 25 percent of touchpoints. This column will be empty if this is a new GA4 installation or if the path only contains a single touchpoint.
- **Mid touchpoints**: During the shopping journey, the middle 50 percent of touchpoints. This column will be empty if this is a new GA4 installation or if the path contains only one touchpoint or only two touchpoints.
- **Late touchpoints**: During the shopping journey, the last 25 percent of touchpoints. If the conversion path only contains a single touchpoint, this column gets all of the credit for conversion.

The user can also change the dimension or the attribution method used in the conversion path reporting. For instance, the user could change from the default of looking at conversions by channel grouping and the cross-channel data driven attribution model, and they can look instead at campaigns using last click attribution.

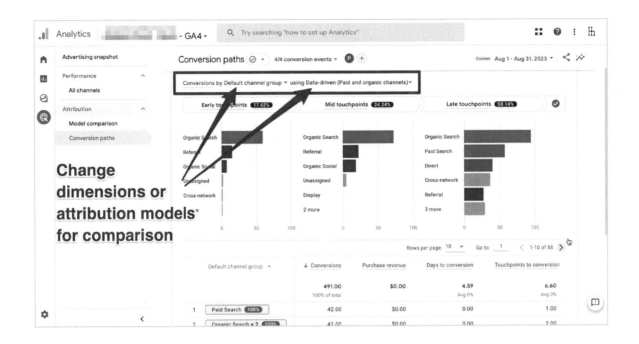

Change dimensions or attribution models for comparison

Admin Menu

Here is a look at the new GA4 admin menu, updated in the fall of 2023. Google redesigned its Admin page for easier navigation and configuration. Settings are now organized into clear categories like Data Collection, Account Settings, and more. Everything related to reporting data is grouped under one section. This categorization allows you to find the right settings quickly with fewer clicks. As a reminder, properties live within accounts. For instance, a dealer group maty have an account for their group, and then have multiple properties, one for each dealer website.

There remains something glaringly missing for GA Universal users, there are no View menus. That is one of the fundamental changes with GA4. There are no longer multiple views available for each website property, but it is speculated that at some point Google will add views to GA4.

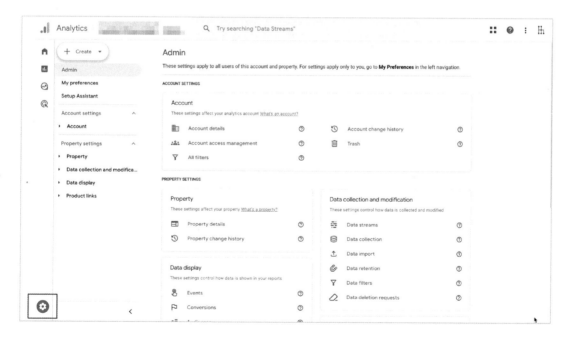

The new GA4 hierarchy is simple as there are accounts and there are properties, and there are no longer views. The account level is the top of the GA4 food chain. Accounts own the properties. The properties are websites or apps or both. User access can be given at either the account level or the property level.

A dealership should consider whether they should grant access at the account or property level. For instance, a dealer group may have stores, so there are several properties within their account and a website for each one. They may work with an agency that only services one of their websites, so they would only grant user access in the property column for that individual website.

Setup Assistant

The Setup Assistant in the property level is a tool for automatically generating the initial GA4 tracking code and data stream.

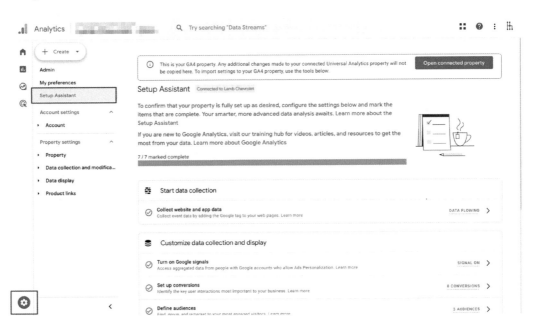

Account Settings

The account level is the highest access level within GA4. Settings made at the account level apply to all properties (i.e., websites) within the account.

Account details

The Account details option in the Account submenu has limited use for dealers. It is primarily to change an account name, and there are various other switches that should be left at their default settings.

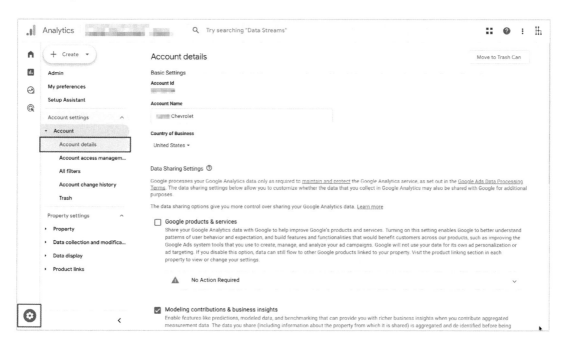

Account Access Management

The Account Access Management option in the Account column allows the dealership to add, edit, or remove GA4 permissions access at the account level. That means anyone added in this section at the account level will have full access to any existing or new properties created in the account. The dealership can also edit the permissions level for any existing users.

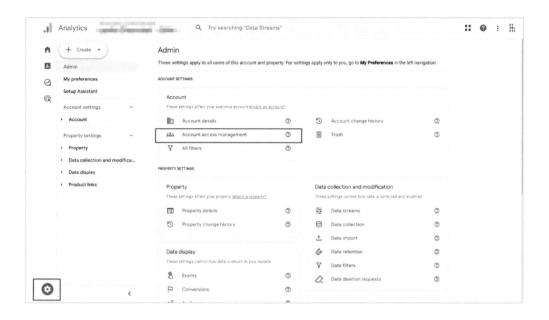

Adding New Users: To grant new users access to an account, the user should click the blue plus sign as shown in the next screen. The system will give a choice to add either users or groups, and the user should select Add users.

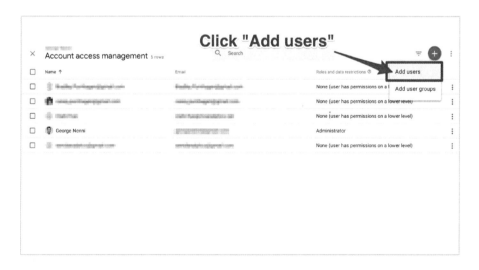

After clicking to add new users, the next screen is presented. The user should first enter the email address for the person who is receiving the GA4 access. Knowing which account-level permission to choose can be tricky.

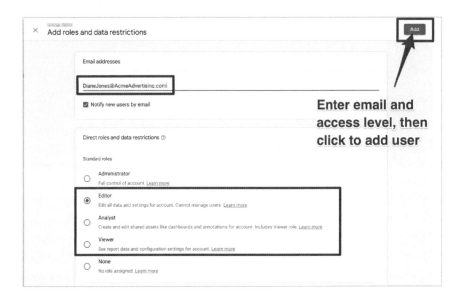

Here is a brief summary of what each GA4 permission level does, keeping in mind that all levels affect each property within the account:

Administrator: Full control of GA4 account, including managing users and editing the account. The dealer should only grant this level of access to dealer ownership or senior leadership.

Editor: Can create, edit, and delete all property assets. Cannot manage users.

Analyst: Can edit certain shared assets.

Viewer: Viewing access only with no editing. If dealers are nervous about granting GA4 access at the account level, this is safest.

Editing or Deleting Existing Users: To edit the access level for existing users, or to delete users, click on any name in the account access management list.

After selecting a GA4 user to edit, the next screen is presented. The user can change the existing permissions level, or they can remove access altogether.

All Filters

The All Filters menu choice in the account level does not apply to GA4, it only shows the existing filters from the properties still running GA Universal.

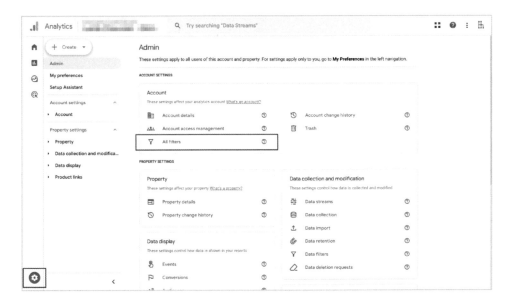

For GA4, filters have moved into the Data Settings menu within the property column. There are two parts to building filters. First, internal traffic needs to be defined, and then the user applies that definition to the filters.

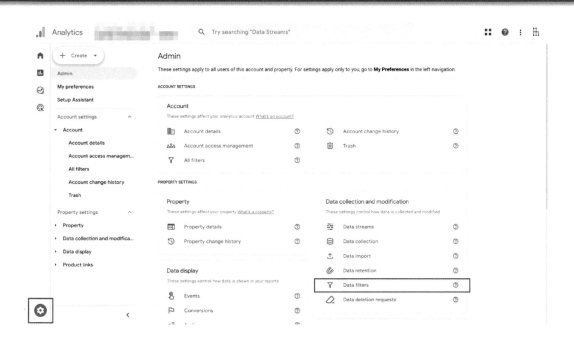

Account Change History

The Account Change History function in the account menu shows a record of changes made to the dealership account.

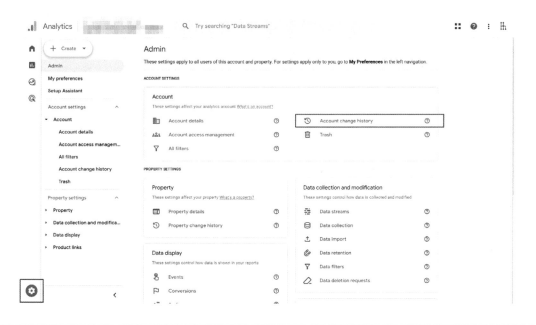

Below is a sample screenshot of the typical information that would be displayed on the account change history report.

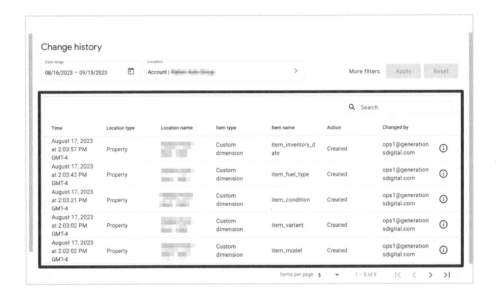

Trash Can

The Trash Can menu selection displays any accounts or properties that were flagged for deletion but are in a temporary staging area before they are eventually deleted. Accounts or properties will be held there for thirty-five days before they are permanently deleted.

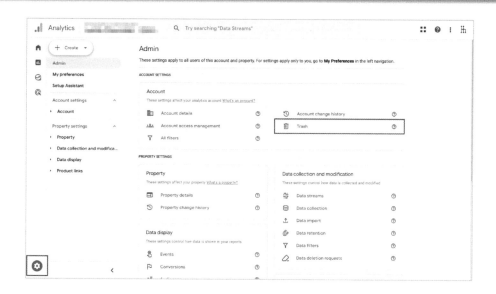

The user can select one or more items that are displayed and, by clicking the restore button, those accounts or properties will be moved out of the trash can. To restore items, the user must have editor-level access.

Property Settings

The property level is the lower level within GA4, and it represents individual dealer websites and dealer apps (if applicable). All properties live within accounts. Some settings can be decided at the account level or the property level. Account-level decisions and access affect all properties, so a dealer should think through whether to switch settings at the account level or at the property level.

Property Details

Property Details contain some basic information about a GA4 property, including property name, industry, time zone, and currency.

The next screen shows a dealership's property details. Once changes are made, the user can click to save them. The screen also contains an option to move a property to the trash can, and that option is in the upper right corner.

Property Access Management

The property access management screens allow a user to add, change, or remove access for users of the particular property.

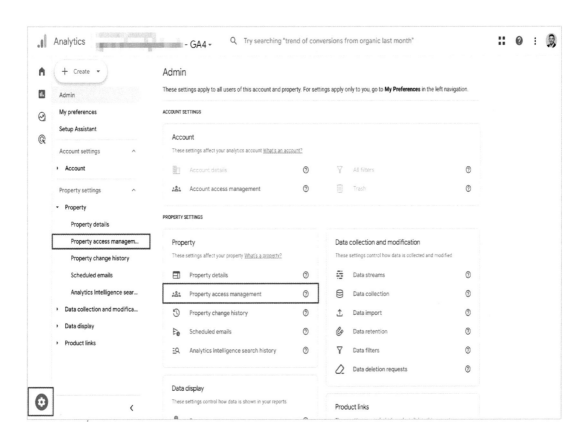

Adding New Users: To add new user access to a property, the user should click the blue plus sign, as shown below. The system will provide a choice for adding either users or groups to a property, and the user should select Add users.

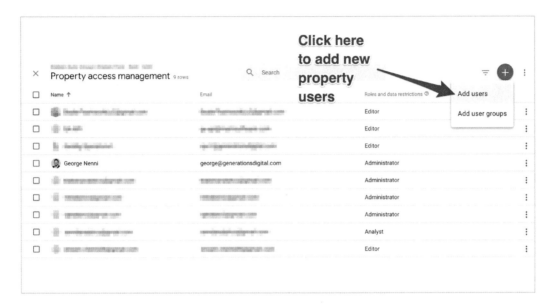

After clicking Add new users, the next screen is presented.

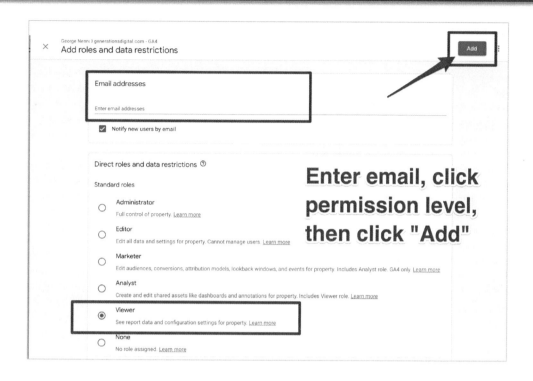

Similar to the process of adding a user at the account level, simply entering an email address and choosing the permission level is all that is required.

As an easy reference, here are the GA4 permission levels again:

Administrator: Full control of GA4 property, including managing users and editing the account. The dealer should only grant this level of access to dealer ownership or senior leadership.

Editor: Can create, edit, and delete all property assets. Cannot manage users.

Marketer: Can create and edit audiences, conversions, attribution models, lookback windows, and events.

Analyst: Can edit certain shared assets.

Viewer: Viewing access only with no editing. If dealers are nervous about granting GA4 access, this is the safest.

Editing or Deleting Existing Users: To edit the access level for existing users, or to delete users, click on any name in the property access management list.

After selecting a GA4 user to edit, the next screen is presented. The user can change the existing permissions level or remove access altogether.

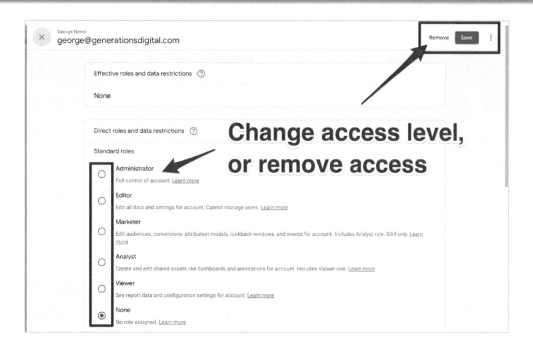

Property Change History

The Property Change History function in the property menu shows a record of changes made to the dealership account.

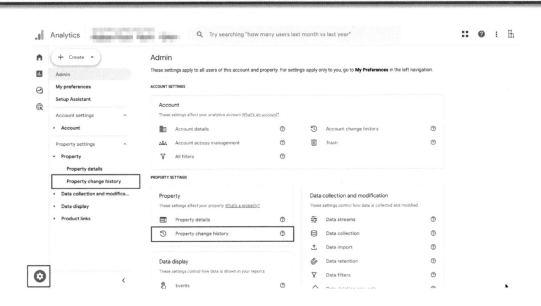

Below is a sample screenshot of the typical information that would be displayed on the property change history report.

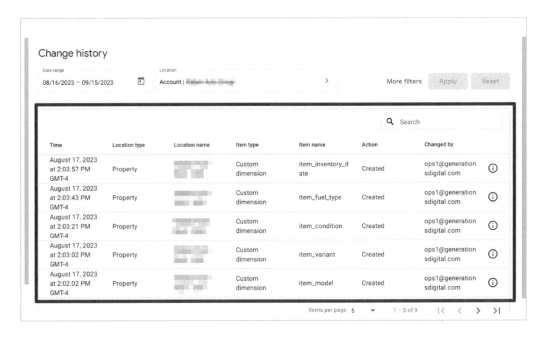

Data collection & modification settings

Data Streams

Data Streams is one of the unique and helpful concepts of Google Analytics 4, in that these streams can come from three places:

1. Dealership website
2. Dealership iOS app (iPhone)
3. Dealership Android app

In addition to data streams allowing users to combine website and app analytics, the data stream also protects the account from spammy traffic injected from unapproved sources. With Analytics Universal, it was relatively easy for a third party to inject fake, spammy traffic data into a dealer's analytics property. This traffic was not real, in that it did not actually visit the website, but created mis-reporting in the dealer's analytics. With GA4, only authorized data sources can pass information into the analytics via the data stream.

Once data streams are set up and data is flowing through a Dealer eProcess, Dealer Inspire, or DealerOn website, there is little maintenance required. There will be times when vendors and agencies may ask a dealer for their measurement-ID, stream-ID, or their G-number. This is one of the places to find that information.

The next screen shows the simple options for either clicking on an existing stream or creating a new one. Let's click on an existing dealer website stream to look at options and other important values.

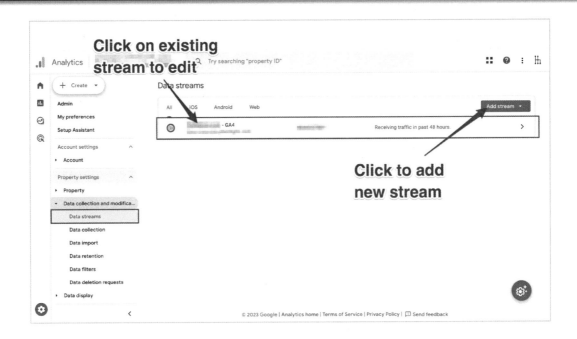

The above screenshot shows a live dealership GA4 website data stream. There is a status showing that the data stream is flowing. There is also the important Measurement ID starting with a capital G, followed by a dash, and then followed by a ten-character alphanumeric ID number. In the old GA Universal, there was a UA-number instead of the G number. Why is this G number so important?

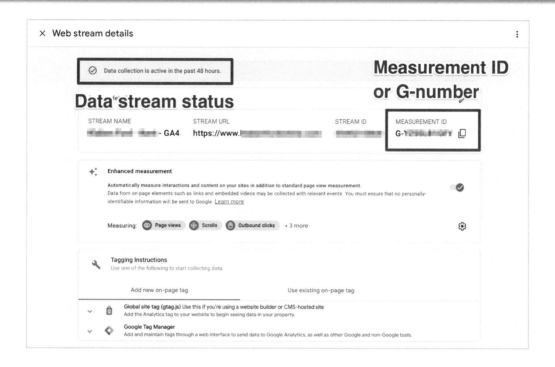

When dealers request that their digital retailing, chat, or trade tool providers start firing GA4 events for conversion tracking, they will need to give their measurement IDs, or their G numbers to those providers. That allows the provider to connect their plug-in tool conversion tracking into GA4.

The web stream details also show which Enhanced measurement events are currently firing on the site based on actual usage. As a reminder, Enhanced measurement events are part of what make GA4 so much better than GA Universal. These new built-in events help the users to track website interactions without any coding or Google Tag Manager work at all.

The user can see more details, and turn Enhancement measurement events on or off, by first clicking on the gear icon.

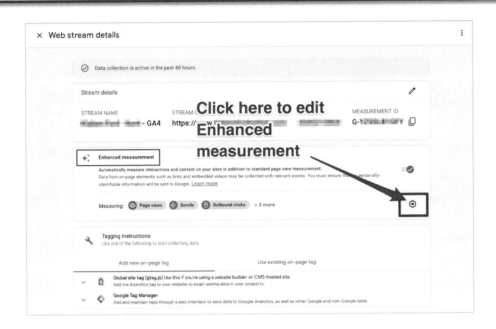

The screenshot below shows more detail on each enhanced measurement, and it allows the user to turn on and off all events except for page views. Once changes are made, clicking save completes the process.

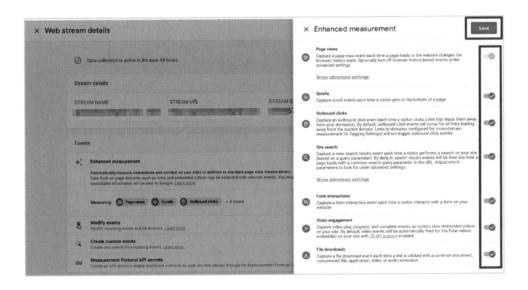

While in the data stream, we also want to check on a default setting, and we need to create a definition for internal traffic. What does a definition for internal traffic mean?

Defining Internal Traffic: The reader may remember that earlier in this book we wrote about the data filtering system in GA4 having changed significantly, and I believe that is an improvement for the better. With GA4, we first need to define what internal traffic is by creating a rule that includes the IP address or range of addresses for internal dealership employee Wi-Fi or wired internet traffic. Once we create this definition, we will use it in the Filter menu that appears later in this book in order to filter internal employee traffic.

The first step we need to do is to define the dealership's internal traffic. While in the web stream details page, and at the bottom of the page, the user should click on Configure tag settings as shown below.

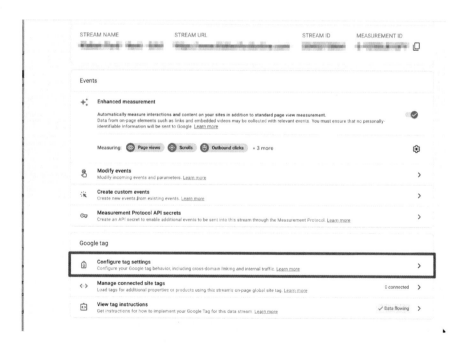

After selecting Configure tag settings, the user is taken to the next screen and is then ready to build an internal traffic definition. We will use this definition later when setting up data filters for GA4. To start the process, the user should click on Define internal traffic as shown next.

After clicking to create the definition, the user is taken to the next screen.

If this is a new GA4 account, it is likely there are no existing definitions. If definitions were listed, the user could click on one to view and edit it. For this exercise, we are going to create a new definition, so we will click on the Create button.

After clicking the create button, the user is taken to another screen. As a reminder, our example will filter our internal dealership wired internet traffic for employees. This is done by telling GA4 to filter out traffic from a single IP address or a range of IP addresses. The example above filters out a range of IP addresses beginning with string: 190.168.1.2

What is an IP address?: An IP address is a unique numerical internet address that identifies a local network. The acronym of IP stands for Internet Protocol, and it is the set of rules that govern the format of data sent across the internet. An example of an IP address is 192.168.1.20. Dealerships are often assigned ranges of IP addresses because they have so many employees and network requirements. For instance, a dealership may have 192.168.1.20, 192.168.1.21, 192.168.1.22, 192.168.1.23, and so on. In that case, we could design a filter to exclude traffic that starts with 192.168.1.2. A dealership should also find out if they have a separate internet router for employees versus customers. If that is the case, the dealer may want to filter out the internal traffic of employees but not the customer Wi-Fi. The network administrator will help the dealer locate the proper IP address or IP address range for potential filtering.

In addition to naming an internal traffic definition, it is important to choose and keep a note of the traffic type value. The default for this is internal, but larger dealers and groups should consider custom naming this parameter if they want to test different filtering definitions, including wired internet, employee Wi-Fi, etc. If a change is made in this screen that changes the default of internal to internal customer Wi-Fi, then the user would make a note of that and use it when creating the actual filter which we will discuss later in this book. Once the appropriate information is entered, the user should click on the Create button.

After clicking the Create button to create the internal traffic definition, the user is taken to the following screen, and they should see the new definition in the list. At this point, internal traffic is now defined for the dealership. We will use this definition later in the book under the Property Menu and under Data Settings and Data Filters in order to filter out internal employee traffic.

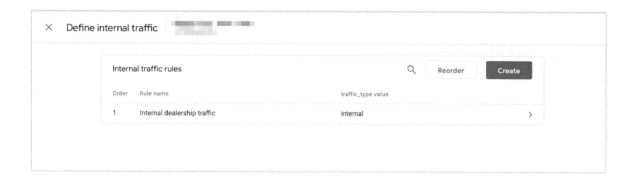

Adjusting Timer for Engaged Sessions: As mentioned earlier, one element in the definition for engaged sessions in GA4 is that the website shopper must stay at least ten seconds. This default can be changed in ten-second increments all the way up to sixty seconds.

While in the expanded Stream tag settings configuration menu, choose Adjust session timeout as shown below.

After choosing Adjust session timeout, the user is taken to the following screen.

As shown above, the user simply changes the default ten seconds to the time of their choosing. We recommend leaving this setting at the default of ten seconds unless engagement rates are unreasonably high.

There are many more functions and settings at the bottom of the web stream details, but they are beyond the needs of most franchised dealers and thus beyond the scope of this book.

Data collection

The Data collection submenu under the Data collection and modification menu contains some important functions for the typical dealer or group. There are a number of settings that we want to make sure are set properly.

In the screenshot below, the switch for Google signals should be turned on, and the switch for including Google signals in reporting identity should be turned off. This was highlighted earlier in the book. Google signals is website traffic that Google links to users who are signed in to their Google accounts and have Ads Personalization activated. This connected data with these logged-in users allows cross-device reporting, cross-device retargeting, and the export of cross-device conversions for paid search integration in Google Ads.

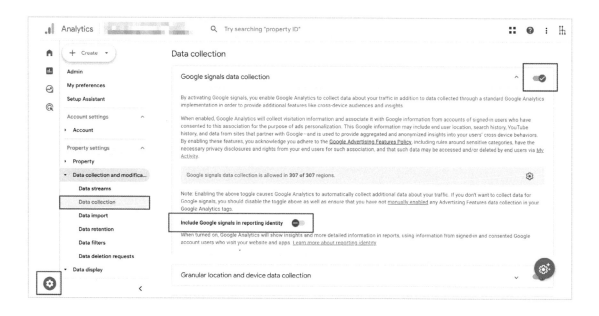

Data Import

The Data Import tool in GA4 allows the user to upload data from external sources and combine that data with GA4. That level of GA4 usage is beyond the scope of normal dealership digital marketing inspection and, thus, is beyond the scope of this book.

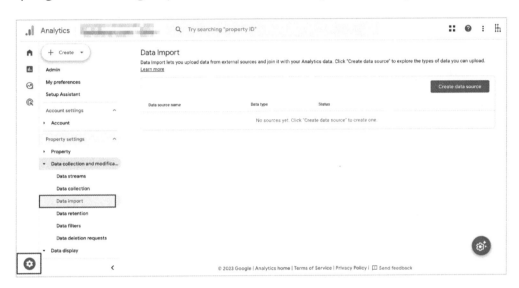

Data retention

The Data retention submenu under the Data collection and modification menu only contains one setting. As mentioned earlier in the book, it is important that dealers change the default setting.

In the next screenshot, we can see that the user has changed the default of two months to fourteen months.

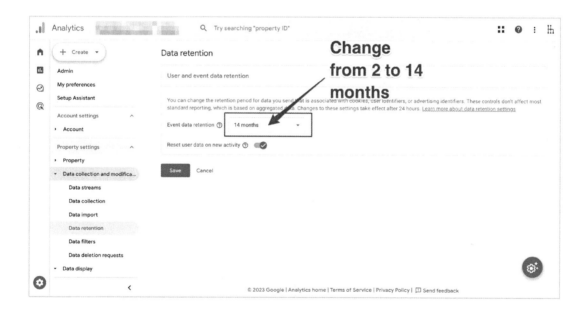

Note: This setting only affects the Exploration reports, and it will not affect the standard reports that are in GA4.

Data filters

The Data filters submenu under the Data collection and modification menu contains the property's filter settings for either including or excluding event data. The user can have ten filters per GA4 property. Filters only begin once they are implemented. They cannot go back in time, and the filtered data is permanent. For this reason, if the dealer or group is using Google Data Studio, then we strongly recommend filtering at that level. Filtering in Data Studio is much more flexible, allowing the user to apply and remove filters on historical data.

As shown in the next screenshot, the user simply clicks to edit existing filters or clicks on Create filter to build a new filter. For our example, we will demonstrate how to filter out internal dealership traffic. The user should first click on the Create filter button to do that.

After clicking to create a new filter, the user is presented with a choice of developer traffic (from iPhone or Android apps) or internal traffic (website). The user should choose internal traffic.

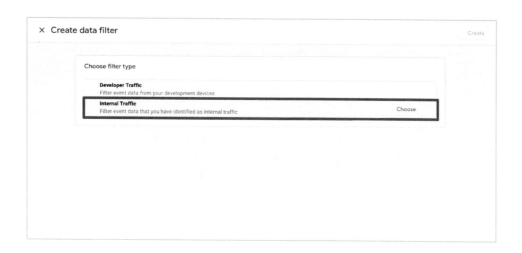

The user is then taken to the next screen to name and build the filter. Once the user has named the filter, they should enter the internal traffic definition/parameter they created earlier on in the Data Stream section starting on page 90. There also needs to be a decision on whether to test the filter prior to making it active. The ability to test new filters is a new function for GA4, and the test data is available as its own dimension. Once the proper information has been entered, a click of the Create button finishes the process.

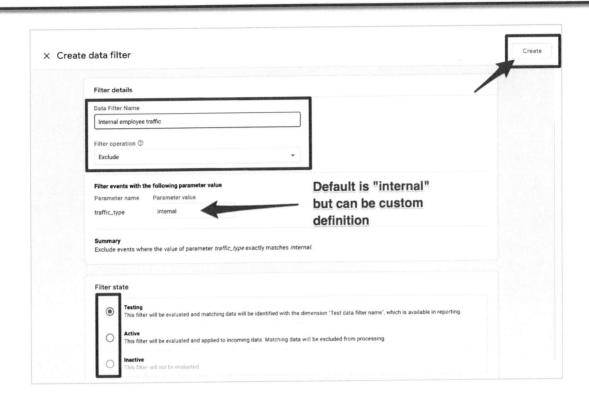

If the user chose to first test the filter, they would be presented with this screen, showing the directions for inspecting the filter test data in its own GA4 dimension.

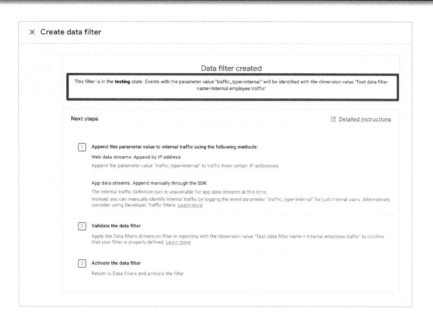

If the user chose to skip testing and simply activate the filter, they would first see a warning message. The user could either cancel the process or click to activate the filter.

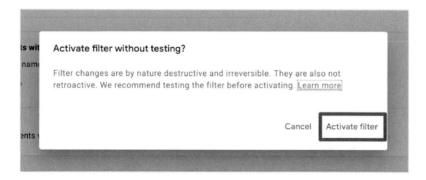

As previously mentioned, since we use Google Data Studio for automotive analytics, we do not recommend filtering in Google Analytics as the data that is filtered is permanently removed. Filtering downstream in Data Studio offers far more flexibility because filters can be applied and removed from historical data.

Data deletion requests

The Data deletion requests menu allows a user to issue a request for data deletion from the GA4 servers with a maximum of twelve allowed at any time. These requests can take anywhere from a week to nine weeks to be completed.

The Data deletion requests report also displays a list of the most recent requests and allows a user to cancel any new requests within the first seven days.

Data display

Events

As discussed in depth earlier in the book, the Events submenu in the Data display menu allows a user to create new events or modify events. For more information, refer back to the chapter on events. The events controlled in this submenu include the default GA4 events, and they include the automatically collected and the enhanced measurement events. The events submenu also creates and modifies any custom events created by individual users.

Below is a look at the default events that GA4 installs for every new website property. As mentioned earlier, those events are tracked automatically and cannot be turned off.

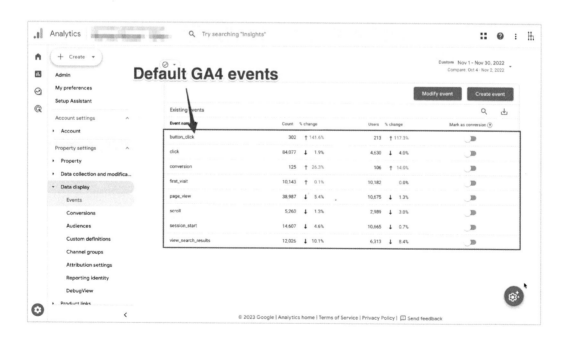

There are two groups of events installed by default: Automatic Events and Enhanced Measurement Events.

1. **Automatic Events**:
   - The page view event shows the website page the user is viewing.
   - The first visit event is triggered automatically the first time a visitor comes to the dealer website. This event is used to calculate New Users in the GA4 reporting.
   - The user engagement event is fired and used to track visitors who spend at least ten seconds on the dealer website.
   - The session start event tracks when a user session starts. Also, a new session start event is triggered when the user has been inactive for at least thirty minutes.
2. **Enhanced Measurement Events**:
   - Scroll: Reporting on visitors scrolling at least 90 percent of a page.
   - Click: Outbound clicks from a dealer's website.
   - Form interactions: Shopper interactions with website lead forms.
   - Video start, video progress, and video complete: Metrics showing shoppers who are viewing website-embedded YouTube videos.
   - File download: Reporting on shoppers downloading content from the dealer website.

In addition to the default events installed on all new GA4 properties, the user can create their own custom events for tracking various shopping or conversion activities. As mentioned earlier, we hope to see more automotive website and tool companies rolling out their ASC standard events in order to make setup and measurement easier and more accurate. Beyond that standard, we feel a key differentiator for automotive website and plug-in tool providers will be their sophistication level with passing parameters for their custom events. These parameters will allow users to create custom dimensions and metrics that are based on elements passed from the dealer website. For instance, the automotive website provider could create a custom event for lead forms and pass the vehicle detail page

URL along with the event. That would allow GA4 reporting on which vehicles the dealership received lead forms.

In the next screenshot, a dealer with an automotive trade tool from TradePending has events firing for both lead forms and mobile click-to-calls. TradePending was one of the first third-party automotive tools to begin firing custom GA4 events,

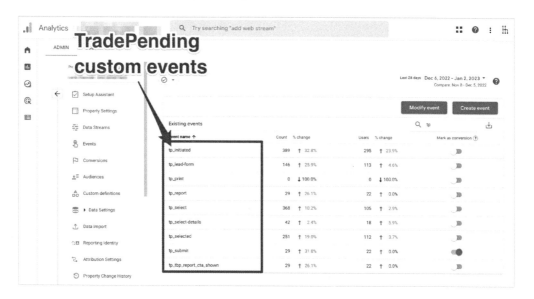

Conversions

The Conversions submenu in the Data display menu allows a user to see any existing conversions, and it allows a user to build a new conversion event. We prefer the method described in the prior section where we observe the events that are firing on the page and there is a slide to mark them as a conversion.

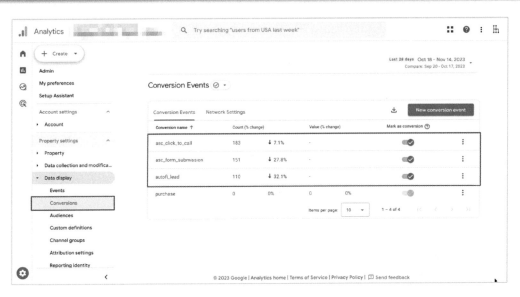

For the purposes of dealer websites, GA4 will automatically mark purchases as conversions, as shown above. The term, purchases, is more commonly used for e-commerce platforms with shopping carts and online transactions which are not yet widely implemented for automotive websites. For this reason, we will ignore that conversion method for now.

Users can also create a conversion event based on an existing GA4 event by using conditionals and parameters instead of coding.

For the purposes of this book, dealers should rely on both their website providers and their third-party website plug-in tool providers in order to fire ASC and other events for tracking as conversions in GA4. As mentioned a few times, we expect to see more automotive website and tool companies rolling out their new GA4 events following the ASC standards. Custom coding or using Google Tag Manager should not be needed by most dealerships in GA4. Google Tag Manager is a free tool that agencies and large dealer groups may use to centralize the tracking scripts for their dealership websites. If larger dealer groups are managing their own Google Tag Manager containers, then they could fire their own GA4-compatible events for tracking as conversions on their websites.

Here is a list of typical true conversion methods we measured for dealers and how dealers would source those events in GA4:

- **Lead forms**: Eventually they will be events fired by website providers like DealerOn, Dealer Inspire, and Dealer eProcess, but dealers can track with thank-you pages for now.
- **Phone calls**: Events fired by website providers for mobile click-to-calls. If a dealer is using Dynamic Number Insertion (DNI), then events would be fired by DNI provider.
- **Messaging engagement**: Events fired by chat/messaging providers.
- **Trade tool leads**: Events fired by trade tool providers.
- **Digital Retail leads**: Events fired by digital retailing (DR) tool providers.

Audiences

The Audiences submenu in GA4 allows users to segment shoppers by traffic source, channels, events, conversions, or other metrics. This functionality existed in GA Universal, but it was accomplished with creating segments and was not very robust. The new audiences functionality in GA4 is much more powerful. It is also dynamic because, as GA4 gets additional data on previous shoppers, those shoppers may or may not stay in the audiences segment.

A user can create both basic and also very complex audiences by using the sequencing functionality that is available. There are some suggested audiences that provide out-of-the-box audiences that can be used as is or easily tweaked. The user can also build a new audience entirely from scratch. The best idea is to play around with the templates provided to get a feel for how the segmenting and sequencing works.

If the GA4 account is linked to Google Ads, then all of the dealer's audiences will be available for use in Google remarketing or look-alike campaigns. That can be very powerful for remarketing to some of a dealership's segments that are engaged the most.

Below is a screenshot of the Audiences menu where you can see existing audiences, or new audiences can be created.

Let's explore building a new audience, using one of the templates in GA4. We will build a custom audience that will track users who first visit the dealer website from third-party classifieds websites such as Autotrader or Cars.com. The user will start by clicking on the New audience button.

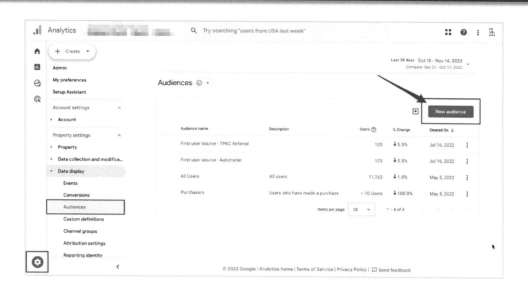

After clicking to create a new audience, the user is brought to the next screen. In this screen, the user can decide to explore some of the Suggested audiences that Google has provided, or they can start from scratch on a brand-new audience. For our example, we are going to edit one of the audience templates.

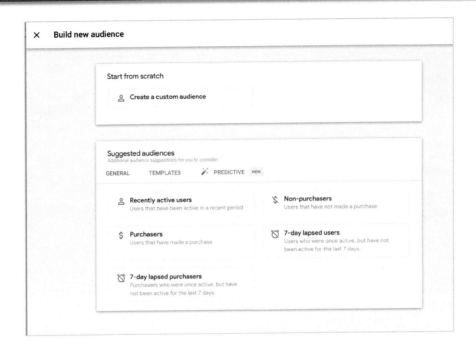

The user should choose the templates tab under the Suggested audiences section. Then the Acquisition template can be chosen.

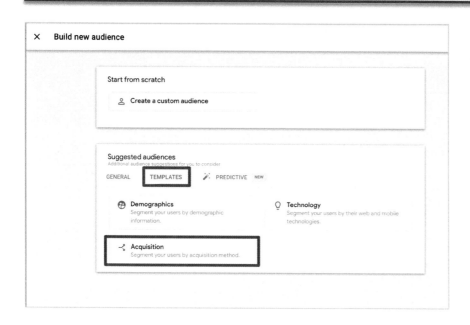

After selecting the acquisition template, the user is taken to the next screen. The user should first name the new audience and then click on the Add filter button.

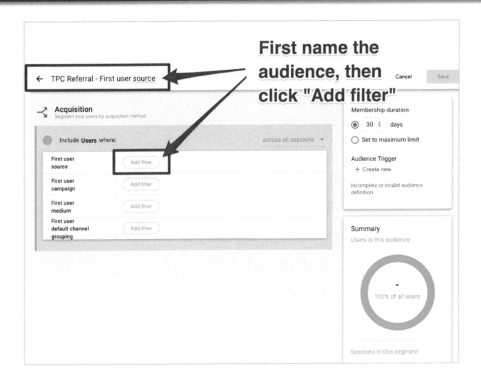

After clicking the Add filter button, the user lands on another screen. To create an audience of shoppers who first visited from third-party classifieds websites, we must create a condition where the source equals a combination of Autotrader and Cars.com referral traffic. By matching the data entered in the above screenshot, the audience will collect any users who first visited from those third-party websites.

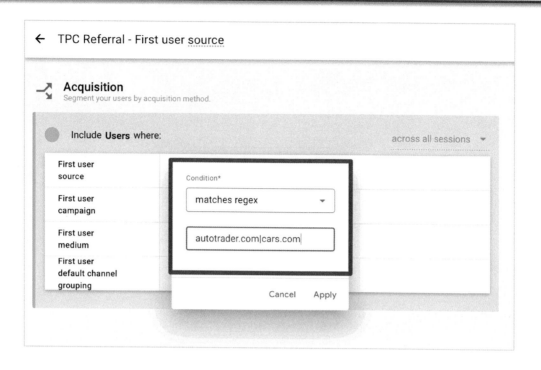

There is a reference above to regex which is an abbreviation for regular expression. Regex is a method using a sequence of characters, along with search string data, that specifies a search pattern in text. The regex above uses a pipe (|) which means "or" in regex. So, the string above looks for traffic sources from either Autotrader or cars.com. This is the most basic application of regex. There is an entire regex language that goes beyond the scope of this book. Google Analytics makes extensive use of regex, so a basic understanding is very helpful. A Google search for using regex will yield plenty of results for learning how to build more complex queries.

Once a new audience is created, it will take some time for data to accumulate. When enough time has passed, the audience data will become more meaningful.

Custom definitions

The Custom definitions submenu in GA4 is an important area to learn in GA4, especially as it relates to the Automotive Standards Council (ASC) event setup. Dealerships need to build the thirty-five custom dimensions for the ASC suggested parameters. Users may also wish to create custom metrics for tracking interesting events in report explorations that they do not wish to mark as a conversion event. Examples would be vehicle detail page (VDP) or search results page (SRPs) events.

As mentioned a few times in this book, dealers wishing to take advantage of the ASC events will first need to create custom dimensions for the thirty-five recommended ASC parameters.

Note: For dealers using website providers, Dealer eProcess, or Dealer Inspire, those thirty-five parameters should already have been created by their support teams. Dealers should verify that and, if not, put in a request.

As of the printing of this book, here is a list of the thirty-five parameters for which ASC recommends dealers create custom dimensions:

- affiliation
- comm_outcome
- comm_status
- comm_type
- currency
- department
- element_text
- element_type
- element_value
- event_action
- event_action_result
- event_owner
- flow_name
- flow_outcome
- form_name
- form_type
- item_category
- item_color
- item_condition
- item_fuel_type
- item_id
- item_inventory_date
- item_make
- item_model
- item_number
- item_payment
- item_price
- item_type
- item_variant
- item_year
- media_type
- page_location

- page_type
- product_name
- promotion_name

The process for building custom dimensions for each of the thirty-five parameters is simple. The user simply creates a custom dimension with a name that matches the parameter name.

From the Custom definitions menu, and with the Custom dimensions tab selected, the user should click on Create custom dimension.

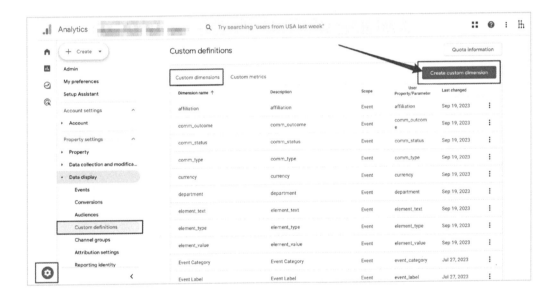

After clicking to create a custom dimension, the user is taken to the following screen.

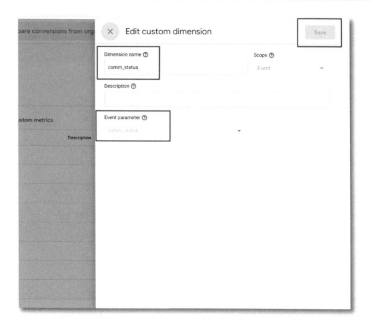

For this example, we are creating a custom dimension for the ASC parameter, comm_status. The comm_status parameter is used by the automotive messaging companies such as CarNow and ActivEngage to indicate where the consumer is in the messaging process. By creating a custom dimension for this parameter, GA4 will allow the user to pivot and report on this new dimension.

Reporting Identity

The Reporting Identity settings are related to GA4's unique ability to measure across devices, websites, and apps. These settings are also very helpful for working around GA4's new data thresholding. More on this below.

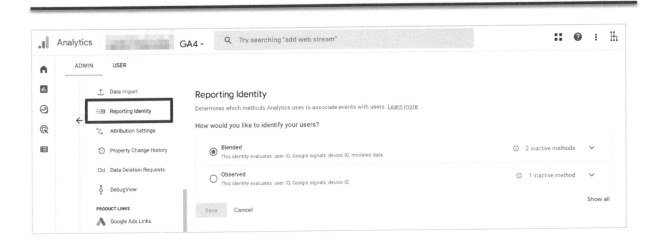

Google Analytics 4 works to combine data from four sources to blend into a single cross-device user journey:

User ID: Most dealer websites receive few regular logins, so doesn't really apply

Google signals: Where available, data from signed-in Google account users that have consented

Device ID: Where available, diminishing with privacy increases

Modeling: Needed to fill the gaps for dealer website reporting

Dealerships today will have limited ability to take advantage of all of the cross-device functionality of GA4. There are many reasons, but there are various blind spots for dealers in cross-device tracking. For instance, nearly every dealer has a website but most do not have dealership apps. The apps would provide additional cross-device activity. Also, most dealers do not have a large percentage of customers who log into the dealer website with a username and password. That is another area of signal loss in automotive, forcing the reliance on other tracking pixels. Therefore, we recommend leaving this setting on the blended method as indicated in the screenshot above. Keep in mind that the option you choose does not affect the way that data is collected or processed by GA4. Dealers can switch between the methods any time without making permanent data changes.

Data Thresholding:

The new GA4 data thresholds were introduced by Google to protect the privacy of individual users by preventing the collection of their identities from demographics, interests, or other signals in the data. If a dealership website has few users during a specific range of dates, and Google Signals is turned on, some data in reports or explorations may not be shown.

When a user views a report or exploration with a narrow date range and very few sessions or events are appearing, it could be that GA4 data thresholds might be applied and that they are hiding some information. To see the hidden data, the user needs to try expanding the date range which could reveal more triggering events. If that doesn't solve the data thresholding issue, the next step is for the user to change the Reporting Identity in order to try and get the hidden data to appear. The process is simple. Once the user clicks on Reporting Identity, they will be taken to the following screen. The user should click on Show all, to expand the menu.

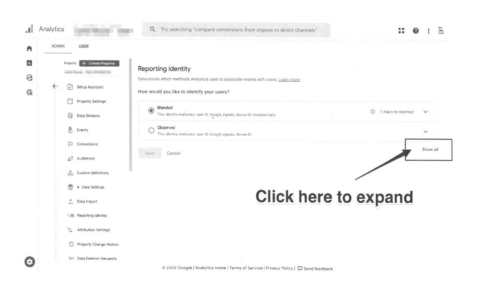

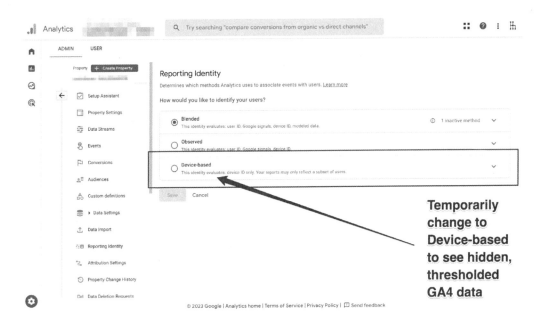

Once the user has expanded the menu, they should see that the current selection is Blended. The user should change that to Device-based and then click save. This is a temporary switch, and users will want to switch back after testing is complete.

Once the user switches to Device-based, they should then check for any missing GA4 events or traffic sources. If users still do not see missing events or traffic after switching to Device-based, they should continue troubleshooting with their agency, website, or plug-in website tool providers.

*New control for Data Thresholding:

As mentioned earlier in the default setting section, Google recently introduced a new setting that will offer the user the benefits of Google signals while limiting the amount of data thresholding that occurs. In order to check and set this default, the user needs to go to the Admin menu and choose the Data Collection submenu within the Data collection and modification menu. The user will be taken to the screen below, matching the setting shown. Users should turn on Google signals by simply sliding the switch on as shown in the screenshot. Users should also turn off the setting for including Google signals data in reporting identity. This combination of settings will limit data thresholding.

DebugView

The DebugView tool in GA4 is used during event building to test, and it requires the user to also run their browser in debug mode to complete the troubleshooting. This level of GA4 usage is beyond the scope of normal dealership digital marketing inspection and, thus, it is beyond the scope of this book.

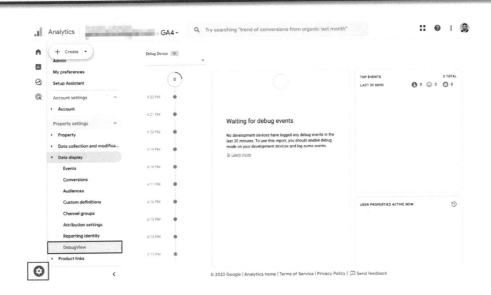

APPENDIX

UTM Tagging Guide for GA4

The new UTM tagging options with GA4 are a significant improvement over what was available through Google Analytics Universal. As a reminder, the current GA Universal stopped tracking new analytics data between July and September 2023.

Why is proper UTM Tagging Important?

Without UTM tagging campaign URLs, all the downstream website click activity will be either partially visible or completely invisible to Google Analytics 4. That means dealers will not know which campaign delivered the best results versus the campaigns delivering poor results.

Setting up Campaign Tracking

Step 1: The dealer should first determine what they want to promote. In the sample case on the next page, the dealer is promoting monthly service specials through an email campaign.

Step 2: Next, the dealer should visit the Google URL Builder website:

https://ga-dev-tools.google/campaign-url-builder/

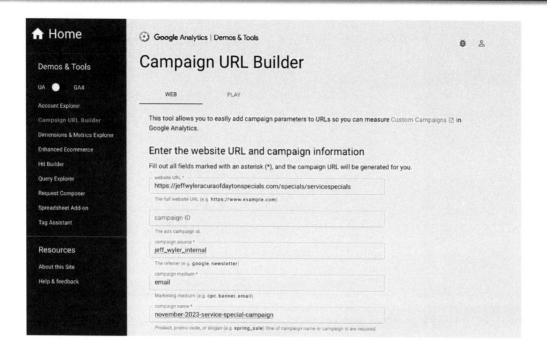

Step 3: Copy the entire URL of the dealership website service specials page, and paste that into Google URL Builder.

https://jeffwyleracuraofdaytonspecials.com/specials/servicespecials

Step 4: Following the screenshot below, the dealership should fill out the rest of the fields, especially the basic ones for source, medium, and campaign name.

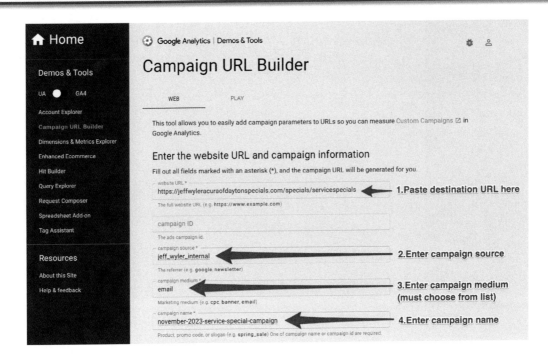

The biggest mistake dealers make is not choosing one of Google's pre-defined mediums. Vendors will often make up their own medium which prevents Google from properly sorting the campaign traffic. UTM parameters also must use all lowercase, and without spaces, using underscores (_) or dashes (-) instead.

Here are some examples:

Campaign Type	Source	Medium
Google Display	google	cpm
Paid Facebook Ads	facebook	paid
Twitter Posts	twitter	social
Email Campaigns	agency_name	email

Here is Google's full list of valid mediums for UTM-tagging with Google Analytics 4:

Affiliates

Medium = affiliate

Audio
Medium exactly matches audio

Cross-network
Campaign Name contains cross-network

Direct
Source exactly matches direct

AND

Medium is one of ("(not set)", "(none)")

Display
Medium is one of display, banner, expandable, interstitial, cpm

Email
Source = email, e-mail e_mail, or e mail

OR

Medium = email e-mail, e_mail, or e mail

Mobile Push Notifications
Medium ends with push

OR

Medium contains mobile or notification

Organic Search
Source matches a list of search sites

OR

Medium exactly matches organic

Organic Shopping

Source matches a list of shopping sites

OR

Campaign name matches regex ^(.*(([^a-df-z]|^)shop|shopping).*)$

Organic Social

Source matches a regex list of social sites

OR

Medium is one of social, social-network, social-media, sm, social network, or social media

Organic Video

Source matches a list of video sites

OR

Medium matches regex ^(.*video.*)$

Paid Search

Source matches a list of search sites

AND

Medium matches regex ^(.*cp.*|ppc|paid.*)$

Paid Shopping

Source matches a list of shopping sites

OR

Campaign Name matches regex ^(.*(([^a-df-z]|^)shop|shopping).*)$)

AND

Medium matches regex ^(.*cp.*|ppc|paid.*)$

Paid Social

Source matches a list of social sites

AND

Medium matches regex ^(.*cp.*|ppc|paid.*)$

Paid Video

Source matches a list of video sites

AND

Medium matches regex ^(.*cp.*|ppc|paid.*)$

Referral

Medium = referral

SMS

Medium exactly matches sms

Step 5: The tool will automatically generate the URL with UTM codes added at the end.

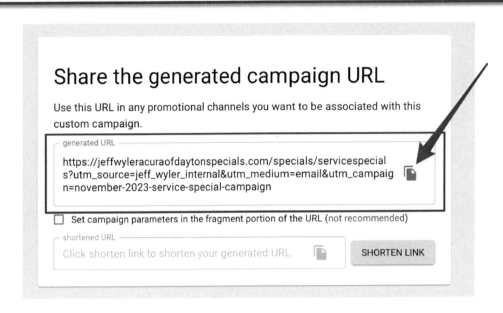

Step 6: If the URL will be visible to shoppers, dealers can shorten the URL in order to create a memorable link across the campaign (email, social, etc.).

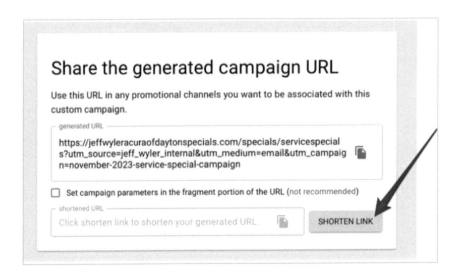

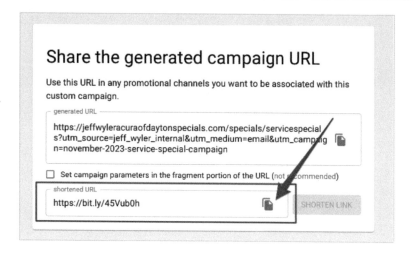

Use the to copy the link.

Step 7: Once the UTM tagged URL has been created in the Google URL Builder, the dealer should first test the tagged URL and make sure it lands properly. If the tagged URL works as designed, then the URL can be used in the email campaign.

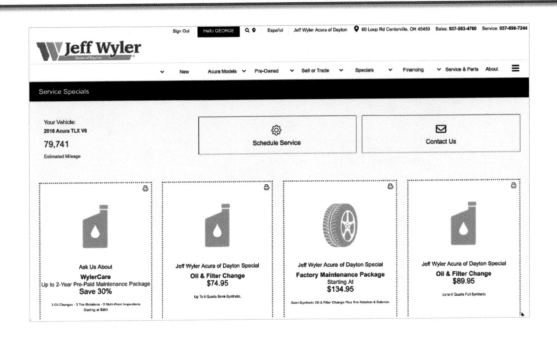

Step 8: Once the email campaign has been running for a few days, dealers can use Google Analytics 4 to easily track the email campaigns.

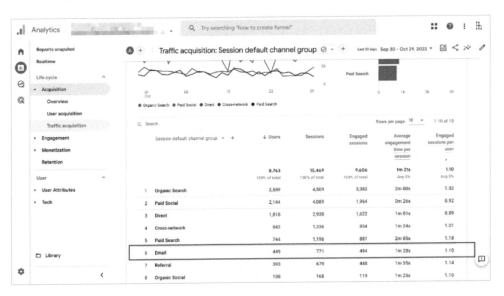

INDEX

ABOUT THE AUTHOR

With three decades of automotive experience, George Nenni educates the automotive industry about emerging technology by writing, speaking, delivering online learning, and sharing his vision for how dealers can maintain a competitive edge. Today, George is the founder of Generations Digital, a technology marketing consulting firm that empowers car dealers to eliminate advertising waste and maximize their marketing dollars. He is also the author of *A Car Dealer's Guide to Digital Marketing*, and *A Car Dealer's Guide to Google Business Profile* all available on Amazon. He is the creator of the popular GMBspy Chrome Extension.

For more information or to contact George directly:

Company website .... https://www.generationsdigital.com

Email .... george@generationsdigital.com

OTHER BOOKS BY THE AUTHOR

A Car Dealer's Guide to Google Business Profile - Second Edition

2022 Amazon Best Seller

"This book is exactly what I was looking for. It took me through the full process of optimizing my GMB/GBP page, and it will be my main reference for any future updates."
(5-Star Amazon review)

A Car Dealer's Guide to Digital Marketing – Third Edition

"An absolutely must-read for the modern car dealership looking to get the most out of their digital marketing investment."
(5-Star Amazon review)

Made in the USA
Las Vegas, NV
15 January 2024

84401967R00107